by the same author

LONDON FABRIC

WEST INDIAN SUMMER

HISTORY UNDER FIRE (with Cecil Beaton)

THE HOUSES OF PARLIAMENT

AMERICA IS AN ATMOSPHERE

MONCKTON MILNES: THE YEARS OF PROMISE

MONCKTON MILNES: THE FLIGHT OF YOUTH

LORD CREWE: THE LIKENESS OF A LIBERAL

ASPECTS OF PROVENCE

THE BATHS OF ABSALOM

QUEEN MARY

QUEEN VICTORIA AT WINDSOR AND BALMORAL

VERANDAH:
SOME EPISODES IN THE CROWN COLONIES
1867–1889

SINS OF THE FATHERS:
A STUDY OF THE ATLANTIC SLAVE TRADERS
1441–1807

HALF-CROWN
COLONY

HALF-CROWN COLONY

A Historical Profile of Hong Kong

BY
James Pope-Hennessy

BOSTON Little, Brown and Company TORONTO

LIBRARY OF CONGRESS CATALOG CARD NO. 73-102186

FIRST AMERICAN EDITION

PRINTED IN THE UNITED STATES OF AMERICA

CONTENTS

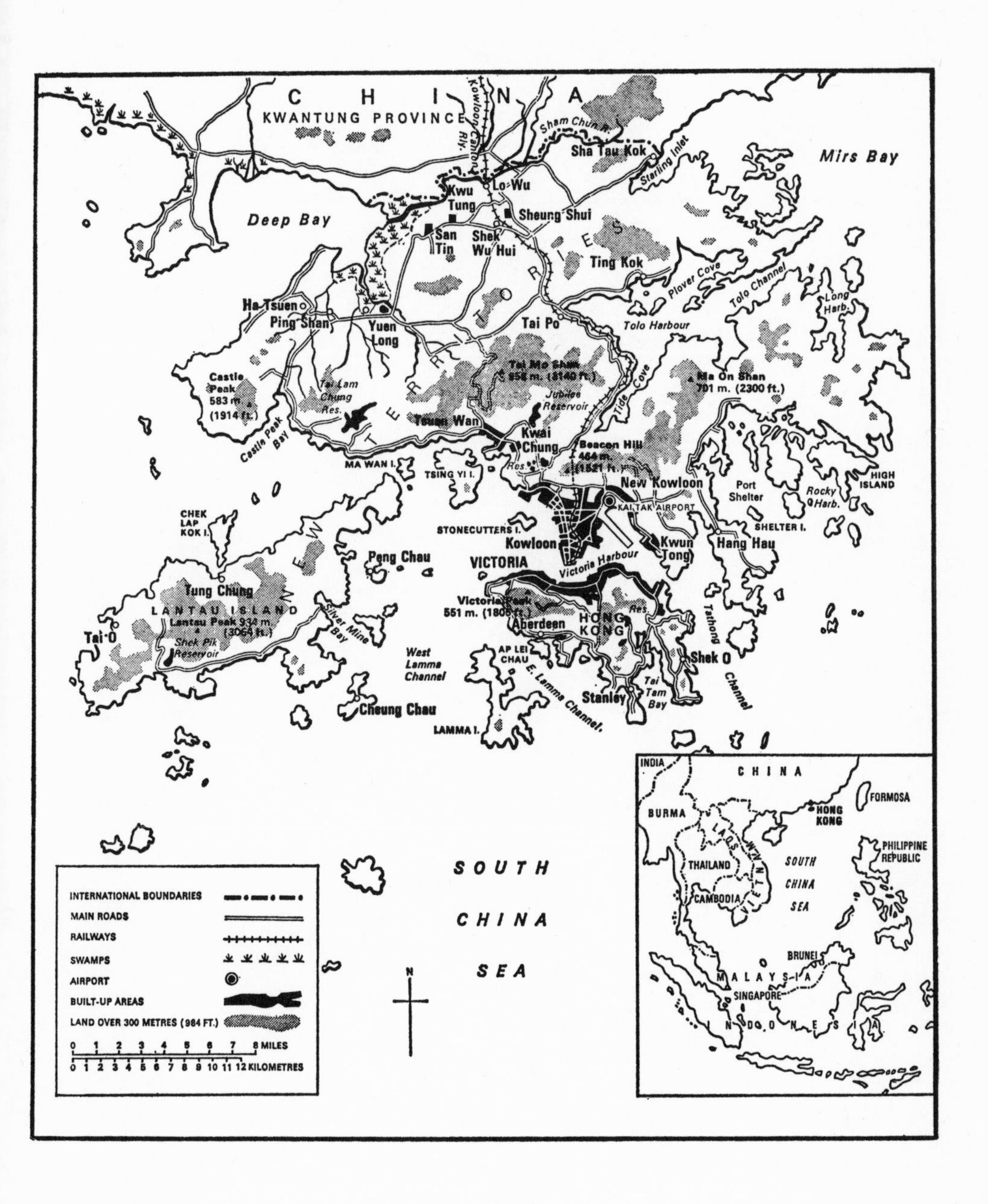

C H I N A
KWANTUNG PROVINCE
Kowloon Canton Rly.
Sham Chun R.
Sha Tau Kok
Mirs Bay
Starling Inlet
Lo Wu
Kwu Tung
Sheung Shui
Deep Bay
San Tin
Shek Wu Hui
Ting Kok
Plover Cove
Tolo Channel
Long Harb.
Ha Tsuen
Ping Shan
Yuen Long
Tai Po
Tolo Harbour
Castle Peak 583 m. (1914 ft.)
Tai Lam Chung Res.
Tide Cove
Ma On Shan 701 m. (2300 ft.)
Jubilee Reservoir
Tsuen Wan
Castle Peak Bay
Kwai Chung
Beacon Hill
MA WAN I.
TSING YI I.
Res.
New Kowloon
Port Shelter
HIGH ISLAND
Rocky Harb.
KAI TAK AIRPORT
CHEK LAP KOK I.
STONECUTTERS I.
SHELTER I.
Kowloon
Kwun Tong
Hang Hau
Peng Chau
VICTORIA
Victoria Harbour
Tung Chung
LANTAU ISLAND
Lantau Peak 934 m. (3064 ft.)
Shek Pik Reservoir
Tai O
Silver Mine Bay
Victoria Peak 551 m. (1808 ft.)
Aberdeen
HONG KONG
Res.
Tathong Channel
West Lamma Channel
AP LEI CHAU
E. Lamma Channel
Shek O
Stanley
Tai Tam Bay
Cheung Chau
LAMMA I.
SOUTH CHINA SEA
N
INTERNATIONAL BOUNDARIES
MAIN ROADS
RAILWAYS
SWAMPS
AIRPORT
BUILT-UP AREAS
LAND OVER 300 METRES (984 FT.)
0 1 2 3 4 5 6 7 8 MILES
0 1 2 3 4 5 6 7 8 9 10 11 12 KILOMETRES
INDIA
CHINA
FORMOSA
BURMA
HONG KONG
LAOS
VIETNAM
THAILAND
SOUTH CHINA SEA
PHILIPPINE REPUBLIC
CAMBODIA
BRUNEI
MALAYSIA
SINGAPORE
INDONESIA

LIST OF ILLUSTRATIONS

LIST OF ILLUSTRATIONS

TO

D. L. SMALL

with appropriate thanks

Its leading characters are wise and witty,
Their suits well-tailored, and they wear them well,
Have many a polished parable to tell
About the *mores* of a trading city.

Only the servants enter unexpected,
Their silent movements make dramatic news;
Here in the East our bankers have erected
A worthy temple to the Comic Muse.

W. H. Auden, 'Hong Kong'

AUTHOR'S NOTE

AS the title of this notebook can hardly fail to indicate, the Crown Colony of Hong Kong is not one of the places on this globe to which I find myself most attuned. Why then, it may well be asked, bother to write about it at all? The answer is that, since working, as an underling, in a West Indian Government House nearly thirty years ago, I have been persistently intrigued by the assumptions and anomalies of British Crown Colony Government. Hong Kong is one of the last surviving examples of such government at work. As the grandson, too, of a Victorian Governor of Hong Kong notorious for his passionate sympathy with what were, in those days, called 'the subject races', I have ever found the arbitrary and optimistic imposition of Western standards on oriental or African peoples a matter of provoking interest.

I cannot say that when I went to Hong Kong in the summer months of 1967 I went with an entirely open mind: I had been there before. But I can at least affirm that I arrived there in a mood of critical detachment. Whilst in the Colony, I was treated with immense kindness and hospitality by friends both old and new. I fear that many of these will not find this book much to their taste, but, as Gertrude Stein once declared, the duty of a writer is to be a witness. We all know that witnesses must not lie.

Hong Kong and London, 1967–8 J.P.-H.

HALF-CROWN COLONY

THE SCENE

TO visit Hong Kong sounds alluring. Indeed the very name was originally a Chinese tribute to beauty—the beauty of a bay. Nowadays the name both of a British Crown Colony and of the rocky island, twenty-nine square miles in area, which forms one of its component parts, the two Chinese words defy acceptable translation into English: 'Fragrant Harbour', 'Perfumed Harbour', 'Sweet-scented Bay'—none of these really works, nor is their implication justifiable today. Once upon a time the island of Hong Kong rewarded travellers with a seductive element of the oriental-picturesque. This has, by now, been pretty thoroughly destroyed.

Along the curving coral beaches of the island of Hong Kong the ebb and flow of the South China Sea deposit those alien objects—thwarted driftwood, odd sandals, empty bottles, discarded hats—which, rejected by the ocean, are returned to land. In the same haphazard way the brief history of the Crown Colony of Hong Kong has been one of a passive acceptance of the adventurers, the wanderers, refugees and speculators who, for more than a century, have drifted to its shores from over the sea. A free port, the very embodiment of the old spirit of let-be, Hong Kong has absorbed these disparate elements—Chinese, Eurasian, British, Portuguese, Jews, Germans, Indians, and anyone else who has happened to see the place in terms of a solution to some personal problem or of an opportunity to grow rich. Generations of British Governors, five-year transients obeying or ignoring the commands of Whitehall, have striven to reconcile the warring interests of commerce and humanity, of education and racial jealousies, and of a bewildering variety of religious creeds. They have tried to impose cohesion and order on a population in its essence inchoate and fluid. Someone has said that the true history of Hong Kong is a mere history of sanitation laws, but, while these have always played a major if largely aspirational part in Hong Kong's seething life, the tale of the British colony is subtler far than that. It might be called, in one sense, a cautionary tale: the cult of money being its central theme. Firms which first made their fortunes in the opium traffic still flourish on the island, although the sources of their wealth are nowadays less destructive and their methods more benign.

Conceived in the old British image and likeness, the Colony of Hong Kong is vociferously inhabited by the Chinese, who form ninety-eight per cent of a total population now nearing four millions. To these it is an emotional involvement and a home. Like many other human concepts Hong Kong is the victim of a number of legends: it is presented as an exotic holiday resort, a shoppers' paradise, a commercial miracle, a triumph for the old liberal principle of free trade. Above all it is promoted as the supremely successful example of East meeting West—a pulsating denial of Kipling's famous lines, a radiant proof of the feasibility of union between two eternally opposed worlds. Is Hong Kong, in fact, all or any of these things?

Before examining this question, it is necessary to take a

long look at Hong Kong itself—the island in its modern context, its scarred green hillsides bristling with the white block-towers of flats, the central area of its capital a monument to the current British ideals of civic architecture today, its lofty tenements where washing hangs motionless in the stuffy air from crowded, rusty balconies. Noisy and scurried the life of Hong Kong is the very antithesis of the *dolce far niente*. Every face seems set on one objective—the making of money—whether it be the millionaire out to double his fortune or the ingratiating, agreeable waiter hovering for his fifty-cent tip. In the thronged streets of Victoria, the capital, every passer-by looks intently dedicated to some private and profitable plan—the tall British at a long-legged stride, the Chinese, elbowing, at the trot. This is no exotic dream city of legend, but a hard-headed community of chinking reality. You can, indeed, almost hear and smell the money in the streets. Hong Kong is a place of the greatest wealth juxtaposed to the greatest poverty—the case, perhaps, in business cities the world over but somehow more salient and more brazen in the East, where so many have so little and where compassion and sympathy stop abruptly at the limits of the family or, sometimes, of the family firm. You cannot stay long in the Colony without becoming aware of a squalor and overcrowding which even the Government's great resettlement schemes seem powerless to defeat.

This, at any rate, is true of the capital city of Victoria and its environs, and of the other congested areas of the island such as Chai-Wan on the north-east coast and Aberdeen on the south. But, like all the islands set within the China Seas, Hong Kong has certain constants of absolute beauty which can neither be destroyed nor denied. These constants, which never cease to beguile the visitor, and to the charm of which even long-term residents are not immune, may be classified as comprising two natural elements, the one static, the other mobile. The static, unchanging element includes the curve of the shore-line, abrupt and sharp and rocky, indented by some of the most splendid bays in the Orient – Deepwater Bay, Repulse Bay, Stanley Bay, Big Wave Bay, Shek O and the rest. To drive at dusk along the sinuous cliff road through Stanley and on round Tai Tam Bay and harbour to Shek O, gazing down at the sea below and out at the offshore islands in the dying light, became for me a daily experience which seemed never the same and never palled. The little islands scattered in the sea are dark and limpet-shaped; in rain they become invisible, sucked back into a whitish mist.

These, then, are the elements of permanent beauty that the island offers – the shore, the bays, the islands that seem floating on the sea. Yet even these would be nothing without the restless, volatile tropical light – not only the dawns and the sunsets, but the constantly glancing changes of light from hour to hour, the great cloud formations which filter or obscure or enhance the sunlight, and the reflections of which seem to deepen the green shallows of the off-coast sea. The sea itself seems, also, for ever changing under the domination of this stern tropical light – sometimes kingfisher blue, sometimes jade green, sometimes almost white or grey. The light of the tropics is dramatic rather than soft or gentle. In summer-time in Hong Kong you cannot for a moment forget that it is the sun which is in charge and often in the tigerish heat of the streets you can sympathize with our nineteenth-century colonial forebears, who frankly regarded it as an enemy, and fought it with solar topees, parasols and umbrellas and, in Hong Kong, by withdrawing to country villas on the dank, misty slopes of Victoria Peak. Martyrs to their urge to make money, they also made the Crown Colony of Hong Kong.

To react instinctively against the current scene there is not sufficient, and to understand Hong Kong's present we must now go back into its past.

1

THE LION'S PAW

I

LIKE Singapore and several other early additions to the British Empire, Hong Kong was acquired, if not precisely by accident, at least with some reluctance. The island was first occupied by the British in January 1841, but was not legally ceded to them in perpetuity until the Treaty of Nanking, signed with the Government of the Manchu Emperor in August 1842 and ratified in June 1843. Lord Palmerston, who was Foreign Secretary at the time of the original occupation, considered it 'utterly premature' to have annexed Hong Kong, which he dismissed as 'a barren island with hardly a house upon it'. Queen Victoria herself is on record as having derided the impetuous addition to her overseas possessions of this bare and oriental rock. 'Albert', she wrote to her uncle, King Leopold of the Belgians, in April 1841, 'is so much amused at my having got the island of Hong Kong, and we think Victoria ought to be called Princess of Hong Kong in addition to Princess Royal.' Such were the inauspicious beginnings of British Hong Kong – to the Foreign Office an embarrassment, to the Royal Family a joke.

This was the reaction in distant London to the annexation of Hong Kong. Interested persons on the spot did not share this scepticism. These were the British merchants trading in Canton. Behind them were years of frustrating negotiations with the Chinese mandarins there, who could let the China trade expand, or harass and limit it, at will. As early as 1836 the *Canton Register*, an English-language weekly founded by the Scottish brothers Matheson and circulating throughout the foreign community in Canton and Macao, had predicted that British possession of Hong Kong might prove a highly paying concern. The *Register*'s contention was that the Portuguese founders of the ancient settlement of Macao had made a fundamental error in settling there at all, and in enforcing strict trading laws.

> If the lion's paw is to be put down on any part of the south side of China, let it be Hong Kong [the *Register* had urged]: let the lion declare it to be under his guarantee a free port, and in ten years it will be the most considerable mart east of the Cape. The Portuguese made a mistake; they adopted shallow water and exclusive rules. Hong Kong, deep water and a free port for ever!

Macao lies at the mouth of the Pearl River, forty miles from Hong Kong. Its muddy, yellow harbour water is of insignificant depth, whereas the bay of Hong Kong is deep, one nautical mile in breadth and practically land-locked. The naval advantages of this bay were obvious, and it was soon found invaluable by the British navy operating during the wars known to history as the Opium Wars, which ended with the cession of Hong Kong.

II

The sad and mystifying tale of the British opium smugglers whose activities involved Great Britain and China in the two wars which in their turn produced the British presence in Hong Kong has been often and deftly told, most notably by Mr Maurice Collis in *Foreign Mud* and more recently by Mr Austin Coates in *Prelude to Hong Kong*. It is sad because, like the history of the Atlantic slave trade, it shows up human nature at its worst, revealing naked commercial greed with its inevitable concomitants – callousness, hypocrisy and corruption. It is mystifying because the Confucian conception of the universe, a creed which governed the thinking of the Imperial Court at Peking, and which saw China as the centre of the world, with every other nation on earth as barbarians who should be paying tribute to this hypothetical world power, is as hard for us to understand today as it was for the British merchants of the eighteenth and nineteenth centuries. When, in 1729, the Emperor Yung Cheung, whose advisers were made anxious by the increasing addiction of the Chinese to opium and by its effects upon them, issued an edict forbidding its import by foreigners, he expected to be obeyed both by his own officials at Canton and by the foreign merchants who were importing the drug. In the event, the opium trade sped on.

A further Chinese objection to the opium trade was caused by the drain of silver out of China into European hands. Mr Coates has, however, conclusively shown that this traditional objection was not as valid as some historians have assumed. He shows, for instance, that at the time of the Napoleonic Wars opium amounted to only one-eighth of

Chinese imports and 'stood far below Indian cotton, and also below English woollens'. He recognizes, all the same, that the opium trade was the cause of 'the bedevilment of Europe's connexions with China', but makes the arresting point that the sudden, widespread addiction of the Chinese people to smoking opium is inexplicable. Introduced into China from Tibet in the first century B.C., opium was then used for medicinal purposes only. The long-standing Indian passion for eating as against smoking opium had never caught on in China, and it was not until the early seventeenth-century Dutch settlers in Java, who smoked tobacco, began mixing a little opium with it in their pipes, that the smoking of the drug in the East really began. Why did the ordinary Chinese people seize upon opium-smoking, then, with such alacrity? Was it, like dram-drinking amongst the poor of Victorian England, an escape from intolerable living conditions? Or did it appeal to that area of the Chinese mind governed by the Confucian belief that appearance is more important than reality? This theory has been put forward, though it is hard to see why a belief commonly expressed by the harsh determination to maintain 'face' should lead into the twilit bypaths of induced hallucination. Here, once more, is another mystery.

What are not mysterious are the economic reasons for European (and, later, American) opium-smuggling into China. The chief commodities which the West wanted from the Chinese were tea and silks; but, since the Chinese Empire was unwilling to open up the country to serious, big-scale trading, believed that the West had nothing to offer that China itself could not provide, and showed only a lukewarm interest in such products as English woollens, it soon became clear to the foreign traders that they should supply the one thing the Chinese people, as against their Government, did emphatically want—opium. Moreover, the East India Company, which ruled India until the Crown took over in 1857, depended on its opium monopoly to finance its trade in China tea. During the Opium Wars of 1839 to 1842 the Company's opium revenue fell to about £300,000; but, once the wars were over and Hong Kong was settled, Capper, the author of *The Three Presidencies of India* (published in 1853), stated that 'at no period of the history of this article has the trade in it to China been carried on so successfully and so extensively as during the last few years.'

While the sale of opium formed such an important part of its revenues, the East India Company, which held a monopoly of British trade with China, did not condescend to smuggle opium, but sold it to 'country traders' at public auction in India. By a complex system of credits the wholesale value of the opium sold by the Company to these entrepreneurs more than balanced the value of their exports from China, 'thereby', wrote Mr Collis, 'setting the China trade on a sound financial basis'. But the disposal of this Indian opium not only benefited the Company and provided money for the development of public works inside India; it was the foundation of very great fortunes amongst the British traders officially allowed, like those of certain other foreign nations, to live in a cramped, strictly demarcated suburb on the water-front of Canton.

For decades before the declaration of war on China in 1839, the British had made attempts to get successive Manchu Emperors to receive an embassy from the King of

England. But, since the Emperors of China regarded all foreign potentates as satellites, and their emissaries as tribute-bearing barbarians, these efforts bore no fruit. In 1834 Lord Palmerston, then Foreign Secretary, dispatched Lord Napier, with an imposing suite, as Superintendent of Trade in China, with instructions to call upon the Viceroy at Canton. The Viceroy refused to receive him as an equal, and Lord Napier returned to Macao where he immediately died. Palmerston's instructions to Napier had contained a typically ambiguous reference to British opium-smuggling: 'It is not desirable that you should encourage such adventures; but you must never lose sight of the fact that you have no authority to interfere with or prevent them.' Although a considerable section of political opinion in England condemned the opium trade as 'discreditable', the Government were only too well aware of its importance to the Indian revenue, and were being speciously lobbied by representatives of the British opium merchants.

The smuggling of opium into China at all would, of course, have been impossible without the connivance of the Canton mandarins. These dignitaries, to whom all foreigners applied the Portuguese name *mandarim* (giver of mandates), were delegated to deal with the barbarian trading community at Canton, were answerable to the Provincial Governor for carrying out anti-opium ordinances of the Emperor, and were one and all involved in a devious web of extorting bribes or 'squeeze' to permit the opium imports to continue. But as the opium trade expanded during the eighteen thirties, the Provincial Governors began to memorialize the Emperor on the alarming spread of opium-addiction and its grave effects on Chinese health and morale. An exceedingly interesting point is that they blamed the people who smoked the opium more than the barbarians, avid for silver, who brought it in. Three of these memorials were submitted by a very remarkable personage, Lin Tse-hsu, the Governor-General of Hu-Kuang, who had stopped opium-smoking in his province first by demanding the voluntary surrender of opium pipes and stocks of the drug, upon which the offenders were forgiven; next by the imposition of the death penalty for recalcitrant addicts. In Hu-Kuang this system had worked, and Lin suggested it should be adopted throughout the country. These three memorials were sent up to the Emperor in the summer and autumn of 1838. On the last day of December of that year Lin Tse-hsu was appointed Imperial Commissioner to Canton, with overriding authority to investigate drug-smuggling and corruption from the Viceroy downwards.

III

Soon after his arrival in Canton, Commissioner Lin demanded the surrender of all the opium aboard the storage-hulks of the foreign merchants. He put pressure on the foreign community by removing their servants, cutting off their food, and confining them to their ships. After considerable negotiations the new British Superintendent of Trade, Captain Elliot, who was stationed at Macao but came up to Canton, agreed to this surrender. Twenty thousand chests of opium were given up and, to the fury of the British merchants, publicly destroyed. Elliot, who was, like Lin, an honest, civilized and capable man, was accused by the foreign traders of cowardice. Meanwhile, a group of opium smugglers, led by the Scotsman William Jardine, had proceeded to London to egg Lord Palmerston on to declare war, as the only means of opening up the China trade.

Palmerston had probably already decided on a warlike policy with China, but Jardine and his friends gave him detailed ideas of how an expedition, from India, should be mounted. His difficulty, however, was that in the humanitarian climate then beginning to prevail in England—abolition of the slave trade and then of slavery itself being two examples—it would be awkward to embroil the country in a war to make opium-smuggling legal. He therefore settled on a more inspiring theme—maltreatment of British subjects in China, insults to the British flag and theft of British goods. In the Commons debate, and despite a stirring speech by the young Gladstone, who accused the Government of turning the Union Jack into a 'pirate flag to protect an infamous traffic', Palmerston carried the day. Yet, even before the debate and before Captain Elliot's latest news could reach England, hostilities between two British frigates and a fleet of twenty-nine Chinese war junks had broken out. They had ended in the defeat of the Chinese. This British victory virtually marks the opening of the First Opium War, and is known as the first battle of Chuenpé.

In June 1840 a British expeditionary force of three battleships, fourteen frigates and sloops, four armed steamers and four thousand British and Indian troops assembled in Hong Kong harbour. Captain Elliot and a cousin, Rear-Admiral George Elliot, had been appointed the Queen's plenipotentiaries. The demands they carried from H.M.

Government to the Chinese Emperor included an indemnity for the confiscated opium, reparation for insults to the Queen's representative and the opening up of further ports to British traders. Compensation for the insults to British subjects could take the form of the cession of one or more islands off the coast of southern China, but this clause might be waived if proper security and freedom to trade were guaranteed to the British. At William Jardine's suggestion, it was indicated to the plenipotentiaries that the islands should be occupied before negotiations began. The harbour of Hong Kong was being used as though it already belonged to Great Britain, and it was from there that the fleet sailed north to attack Chusan Island. The British force succeeded only in capturing the island's capital, Tinghai, and was unable to occupy the whole of Chusan. Crippled by disease, the British held out in Tinghai while Captain Elliot conducted negotiations with the Chinese who, after a second sea battle, asked for the return of Chusan, and offered Elliot Hong Kong and the value of the confiscated opium. A preliminary treaty was initialled on January 20th, 1841, and, five days later, without waiting for official approval from London, a British survey party landed on the island, raised the British flag and drank the Queen's health. Meanwhile, the Emperor of China had repudiated the agreement. The result was a complete Chinese rout at the third battle of Chuenpé, which left Canton at the mercy of the British. Just before the final assault on Canton, the terms of a new treaty were announced.

When the draft of the Treaty of Canton reached London, Palmerston was enraged. The British found that they had given up Chusan and accepted Hong Kong as a place of trade, but on the understanding that taxes on commerce there would be paid to China. This conditional possession of an island and harbour that the Foreign Office did not particularly want caused Palmerston to berate Captain Elliot: 'You have disobeyed and neglected your instructions,' he wrote to Elliot. 'You seem to have considered that my instructions were waste paper which you might treat with entire disregard, and that you were at full liberty to deal with the interests of your country according to your own fancy.' To the delight of the China Trade merchants, who had long regarded Elliot as being weak and pro-Chinese, Palmerston dismissed him. His replacement was Sir Henry Pottinger, a soldier and explorer with Indian experience behind him but no knowledge whatever of China. War broke out again, Shanghai was occupied and the southern capital of China, Nanking, was invested. To save that city the Chinese accepted, in August 1842, a much sterner treaty than the Treaty of Canton. Under the new terms, which included a substantial cash indemnity, the Chinese agreed that, in addition to Canton, the four ports of Amoy, Foochow, Ningpo and Shanghai should be opened to British traders, with a resident British consul at each. By this treaty, which, we may recall, was ratified in June 1843, Hong Kong passed unconditionally and for ever to the British Crown. Its first Governor was the man who had made the new treaty, Sir Henry Pottinger.

IV

Once Hong Kong had been definitively acquired and declared a Crown Colony, it was realized that, from an administrative point of view, the island would have to be treated as a unique case. 'It follows', wrote Sir Henry Pottinger, 'that methods of proceeding unknown in other British Colonies must be followed at Hong Kong.' What exactly did he mean?

To begin with, Pottinger obviously meant that there was no precedent for the annexation of a fragment of the Chinese Empire, itself a huge, amorphous and arcane power about which little was known politically save that it exhibited a total contempt for every other nation in the world. He also meant that to conjure up a Crown Colony from a bleak rock was a novel, and might prove a foolhardy, experiment. The Crown Colony of Gibraltar, first fortified in the eighth century and having a long history of civilizing Spanish rule until its seizure by the British in the reign of Queen Anne, offered no historical analogy. The nearest colonial case in any way resembling the creation of Hong Kong might have been thought to be the East India Company's acquisition of the fishing hamlet of Singapore in 1819 – but in fact this quickly growing city had at first been administered from Bengal, and was afterwards merged, in 1826, into the new Crown Colony of the Straits Settlements. In any case, the British vision of Hong Kong as specifically a free port, and the fact that it thus not only attracted reputable and wealthy European merchants but also became a magnet for 'criminal elements' from Canton as well as for the wandering riff-raff of the China seas, rendered complex that knotty and vital problem, the maintenance of law and order. Further, there was the question of what line should – or, rather, could – be taken on that most lucrative aspect of the China trade and one to which the new colony owed its very existence: the traffic in opium. From Whitehall, Pottinger was merely advised that he should 'perhaps impede' the opium trade 'in some degree by preventing the Island of Hong Kong or its neighbouring waters from being used as a point whence British smugglers shall depart on their illegal adventures.' The new Governor was personally opposed to the opium trade, but he felt that to forbid the import of opium into Hong Kong would only drive the opium traders elsewhere on the China Coast. All the same, he did issue a stern edict forbidding the smuggling of the drug to or from Hong Kong. This edict proved about as effective as King Canute's orders to the ocean waves.

> The Plenipotentiary has published a most fiery proclamation against smuggling [wrote James Matheson, one of the founder-heroes of the colony], but I believe it is like the Chinese edicts, meaning nothing and only intended for the Saints in England. Sir Henry never means to act upon it and no doubt privately considers it a good joke. At any rate he allows the drug to be landed and stored at Hong Kong.

Matheson, like his partner William Jardine, was a cynic. Indeed, the cynicism of the opium smugglers who became the merchant-princes of old Hong Kong was quite equal to that which animated the former European slave-traders in Bristol or Liverpool, in Amsterdam or Nantes. Unlike the slavers, who were at least supplying an existing demand for plantation Negroes, the opium traders deliberately set out to extend and encourage a national addiction to the drug they wished to promote.

> The *Gazelle* was unnecessarily detained at Hong Kong in consequence of Captain Crocker's repugnance to receiving opium on the Sabbath [wrote James Matheson during the infancy of the new Crown Colony]. We have every respect for persons entertaining strict religious principles, but we fear that very godly people are not suited to the drug trade. Perhaps it would be better that the Captain should resign.

Sir Henry Pottinger's successor as Governor of Hong Kong, a distinguished sinologist named Sir John Davis, gave up the struggle against opium. Finding it absolutely impossible to control the drug traffic through the Colony, he concluded that it had better be legalized, taxed, and turned into a source of local revenue. He set up an unsuccessful opium monopoly or 'opium farm', which was sold to the highest bidder, and, when this system failed, he devised a licensing system by which licences to sell raw opium, to refine and sell prepared opium, and to open an opium den were sold at a fixed rate in Hong Kong dollars. At least one member of Davis's Council protested against 'taxing vice for revenue'; but by this time Hong Kong's position as a major opium mart had become so outstanding that it would have been folly to ignore so rewarding a source of government revenue. Sir John Davis reported to London in 1844, the year of his arrival in the new Colony, that 'almost every person possessed of capital who is not connected with government employment, is employed in the opium trade.' By the next autumn there were eighty Hong Kong clippers carrying opium. Nineteen of these belonged to the firm of Jardine Matheson, the 'Princely Hong'.

Looking round modern Victoria today it is curious to reflect that the men who founded the prosperity of this mundane granite citadel, with its down-to-mud values and air of solidity, first made their money by the sale of that most intangible of all commodities—illusion: for the opium trade, we may infer, provides the only example in mercantile history of massive and prosaic fortunes being made by selling the material for hallucination and artificially induced happiness. Gazing at the hard, shrewd, arrogant faces of James Matheson and the other British merchants whom George Chinnery painted, it is hard to associate these men with their basic role in Chinese nineteenth-century life—that of pedlars of dreams.

2

POPPY DAYS

I

DESPITE the efforts of certain humanitarian governors, the opium trade which was responsible for the founding of Hong Kong continued to nourish it for generations. By 1906 the trade was worth over five million pounds, whilst the revenue from opium licences and from licensed 'divans' or smoking-halls brought the local government over two million Hong Kong dollars. The use of opium in the Colony was not finally made illegal until the Second World War. But if, leaving history aside for a moment, we take another glimpse at the scene in contemporary Hong Kong we shall find that drug-addiction remains a major problem there.

Believers in the questionable concept of poetic justice, or, alternatively, in the irony of history, might be tempted to recognize one or other of these in the modern Hong Kong Government's drug problem. And indeed, in one sense, the wheel has turned full circle. Instead of going out of Hong Kong into China under British auspices, narcotics are now flowing out of China into Hong Kong. A colonial administration, the revenue of which was for decades supported by opium sales, is now obliged to spend thousands of dollars each year on anti-narcotic documentary films and other forms of propaganda. An examination of this point seems relevant here.

'The great majority of all crime in Hong Kong derives in one way or another from narcotics.' This statement in the official *Hong Kong: Report for the Year 1966* is followed by a brief account of seizures of narcotics in that year by officers of the Police Narcotics Bureau, including a consignment which was hidden in specially constructed refrigerators and had a retail value of 17,000,000 Hong Kong dollars (approximately £1,400,000). The general theory, based on ten years' experience by the Narcotics Bureau officers, is that there are some eighty thousand addicts in the Colony, fifty thousand of them on heroin and thirty thousand users of opium.

Against this depressing and almost insoluble problem the Government struggles, using the detective Narcotics Bureau on the one hand, and the curative centres on Sha Chau Island and at Castle Peak in the New Territories on the other. But the smuggling of morphine (to be converted into heroin) is peculiarly difficult to detect, the narcotics squads are understaffed and a number of the latter are said to be wide open to that bribery and corruption freely alleged against junior members of Hong Kong's underpaid police force. Moreover, as is medically recognized, cured addicts are not only vulnerable to re-addiction, but in Hong Kong find it hard to get jobs when they emerge from their clinics, and to adjust again to the fusty conditions of tenement or squatters' hut life.

'I hope you're going to write about the drug addicts here,' someone remarked to me with an almost salacious glee. But, except to its addicts, there is nothing exciting or sensational about the massive drug problem of modern Hong Kong. It is an infinitely sad situation of which the normal tourist is kept unaware both because the addicts and pedlars do not, for obvious reasons, frequent the more touristic areas of the city, and because the addict is only identifiable to the experienced eye. In the more sordid, shadowy alleys of Wanchai, behind the streets of brightly lit bars and restaurants, it is stated to be 'possible for a fairly competent observer to recognize upwards of twenty addicts in a ten-minute walk'.* And it is not only adults who are affected. The children of Wanchai, many of them with an addicted parent, may begin taking drugs themselves as early as ten years old, are used by drug pedlars to carry drugs (since small children are seldom searched), and end up in prison after picking the pockets of drunken sailors or snatching bags or pocket-books from unwary nocturnal sight-seers. The false and superficial gaiety of the main streets of Wanchai, where the young pimps sit on chairs under the arcades raucously inviting you into this or that bar, conceals a whole catalogue of the melancholy and indeed atrocious facts of the life of the poor in Hong Kong, where people sleep in alley-ways and on the rooftops and even, in some cases, consider the stairway of a tenement block their home.

I have earlier quoted Mr Austin Coates as asserting that the spread of opium-smoking amongst the mainland Chinese in the nineteenth century was unique among

* From *Under the Rug: the Drug Problem in Hong Kong*, a singularly objective study in applied sociology by Michael G. Whissen. To this admirable analysis I am indebted for many of the facts in this chapter.

nations and inexplicable. There is, however, a recent theory which suggests that the political turmoils inside China, the civil wars, the changes of regime, the spate of refugees and the general disruption of the old 'extended family' life based on highly rigid and protective principles, may have led to such a state of mental confusion, such a gap between Confucian belief, social appearance and new, hideous realities that for many men the only psychological solution was to throw in their hands and to withdraw into the dream-world of opium. Be this as it may, there is no doubt that the housing conditions of the majority of the population of Hong Kong make – I quote again from *Under the Rug* – 'the idea of a man spending a quiet evening at home with his family ... ludicrous in the context of most homes'. Even in the re-settlement areas, with one family to a room, family life is claustrophobic and noisy; while in the backstreets of Victoria and Kowloon the old houses are still divided and subdivided until it has been estimated that 'a typical family of five may easily pay a fifth of a weekly income of less than four pounds for a windowless cubicle eight feet square'.* A man who wants to get away from it all – away from the strangulating congestion and the direst poverty – shuffles off to a mahjong school or some other gambling place in which he is almost certain first to lose his money and then to fall deeper and deeper into debt; a situation to which opium-smoking appears to him to offer a relief. There is no real opportunity for employing leisure, even if the working members of the family had the time – which is, by and large, improbable. The open spaces, which have

* From *John Stuart Mills' Other Island: A Study of the economic development of Hong Kong*, by Henry Smith.

been imaginatively planted as parks and playgrounds, become dangerous after dark, the haunts of young criminals who are members of a debased form of the old triad societies, and who enjoy introducing neophytes to the pleasures of heroin. There is, in fact, in the poor quarters of Hong Kong, every incentive to escape from reality through the use of narcotics. The increasing hold of these naturally creates in their victim a need for more and more money, at the expense of his family, and finally of his own food. Eighty thousand addicts in Hong Kong is indeed a high figure, but it seems on the whole surprising that there are not a good many more. It says much for the strong-mindedness of the Chinese, even when living in a truncated family group rather than in the old 'extended family' in which the role of each member was clearly defined and understood.

Nor is life for the successfully cured easy. If the family take him back, they will in many cases keep him locked in the room and only allow him out under supervision. Should he try to escape they feel that their worst fears of his re-addiction are confirmed. His self-respect and health restored by treatment, he sets out to find a good job. Should he succeed at this, both his employers and his colleagues will watch him narrowly, will assume that he has been smoking again should he be late, and will tend to suspect him of any casual theft or loss in the factory in which he works. The industrialization of Hong Kong, where employers demand quick returns, pay low wages and know that any of their workers can be immediately replaced from the vast reservoir of the unemployed, means that a cured addict stands small chance of avoiding one, usually fatal, relapse.

II

The precise geographical sources of the raw opium which provides the pabulum of Hong Kong addicts, and others the world over, is, apparently, difficult to establish with certainty. The conviction of some American politicians that the export of opium from Yunnan and Szechwan is but one aspect of a devilish world-plot by Communist China to weaken and destroy the West is supported only by the government of Formosa. It is, rather, to be conjectured that while some opium does enter Hong Kong from Yunnan and Szechwan, most of it comes from the Shan States of Burma, an area over which the Rangoon government has only a slender control, and from the remoter areas of Thailand and Laos. The methods by which it then reaches Hong Kong are numerous. The packaged opium or morphine can be brought overland to Bangkok, Singapore and Penang, and thence shipped to Hong Kong. If vessels are coming to Hong Kong from black-listed ports they can carry their morphine on to Japan, across the Pacific to some innocuous American port, and then bring it back from there. Since opium smells stronger than morphine, and is also bulkier and less profitable, morphine is a more popular import, as it can be concealed in bales of wool or other merchandise. Also, sealed and water-proof packages can be dropped from a small ship or a charter aeroplane in international waters off Hong Kong, to be retrieved by fishing-junk. This last method sets a real poser for the narcotics squad, since one patrol launch may have to cover an area simultaneously afloat with some fifty junks and sampans. Moreover, since the free port of Hong Kong

Ceremony at the cession of Hong Kong Island to the British January 1841

The first fort on Kowloon Peninsula, *c.* 1845

(*below*) The case of the poisoned bread, January 1857. The accused baker Cheung Ah-Lum (standing, full face), his father and other members of his family being examined at the Police Office, Victoria, on the charge of attempted mass murder

(*above*) British and Chinese plenipotentiaries signing the Treaty of Nanking, August 1842
(*below*) Sir John Bowring, Governor of Hong Kong, 1854–9, sketched in the smoking-room of the P. & O. steamship *Hindostan* on his way to take up his appointment

'Roughing it in the Far East', showing the pleasures and hazards of attending an open-air ball on the Peak, 1888

handles twenty million tons of shipping a year, even the most honest and conscientious of customs inspectors cannot winkle out every potential hiding-place in every single ship.

Once safely in the Colony, the opium and morphine are taken over by syndicates—large syndicates in the case of opium, 'smaller and more compact' ones for morphine. These syndicates would seem to follow the usual Hong Kong pattern of concentrating on large, speedy profits: it has been estimated that a well-run opium syndicate would be making fifteen hundred Hong Kong dollars a day. Since the preparation of opium, like the raw material itself, has an unmistakable smell, the steaming of it is conducted in distant parts of the Colony, preferably on chicken or pig farms where the natural stink of the farmyard serves as a cover for the opium fumes. The manufacture of heroin from morphine is more skilled and needs the supervision of a technician, enough space for the equipment, a clean water supply 'and preferably some source of power from which to operate a pump and some means of dispersing the fumes from the acetic anhydride and the ether which are used in the processing'. Such heroin factories have been found in many parts of the colony, and 'located in such diverse places as quiet farms in the New Territories and bathrooms in luxurious apartments'. It will be seen that the lot of the Narcotics Bureau officers is not a facile one, particularly when the possibility of making large sums of money by accepting bribes is offset against the labour of detection.

Heroin, neatly tied into small packages of different shapes and colours to indicate the quality of the contents, is sold at established or mobile street selling points or 'sites' in Victoria or Kowloon. Opium is dispensed to addicts in selected squatters' huts, which have two or three doors for swift exits if the look-out man senses an approaching police raid. Called 'opium divans', they have the traditional two-tier shelf of Gustav Doré's Chinatown engraving, and these shelves or platforms, usually linoleum-covered, sport wooden head-rests. For security purposes the divans tend to be situated in groups. To ensure that the Narcotics Squad does not become too active from disappointment at not having made many arrests lately, the proprietors of the divans are believed to arrange a successful token raid on a fairly empty establishment, let themselves be arrested, go on bail, plead guilty and pay a nominal fine. Apart from the heroin sites and the opium divans, another profitable investment for the narcotics syndicates is provided by the extensive, gang-run drug trafficking within the walls of Hong Kong's convict gaols and ordinary prisons.

Except for the cases of real addiction, it seems to me questionable whether the opium habit, well regulated, is any more harmful than the conventional use of alcohol by the West. Heroin is clearly another matter: and, according to the recent statistics I have quoted, it is heroin that is more and more destined to erode the already threadbare family life of many of the poor in the Crown Colony of Hong Kong.

3

PRELUDE TO KOWLOON

I

'NO historical monument has been discovered on the island,' a resident of Hong Kong wrote in a volume published some thirty years ago: 'nor is there any tradition among local Chinese of stirring events having been enacted here or any suggestion that the island had in the past attained a state of greater prosperity and importance than that in which Englishmen found it.' Nothing, then, to excavate? Yes; but there is one feature of present-day Hong Kong which is, and will presumably remain, of extreme archaeological interest. I refer to its constitution.

Here in Hong Kong we may, at our leisure, study nineteenth-century imperial methods preserved in amber. Despite the relentless whine of jet airliners landing at or taking off from the airport at Kai Tak, despite the model factories, the banks and offices and new hotels on Hong Kong Island or the frugging in the coolest nightclubs of Kowloon, the Crown Colony of Hong Kong lies as firmly moored in the past as the famous floating restaurants of Aberdeen are tethered in the polluted waters of Shek Pai

Wan. The rigid sentry in his sentry-box at the gates of Government House has always seemed to me symbolic of this state of political immobility. And of comfort to the connoisseur of outmoded constitutions is the fact that, unlike other former British Crown Colonies now free, there can never, in the nature of things, be any intention of granting Hong Kong independence. A place which is not a country but a mart, inhabited by a foreign population which has no specific sense of its own identity and only a very pliable one of loyalty to the Queen, and which, once free, would be reclaimed by China overnight, cannot conceivably be made into a nation. The present Governor of Hong Kong is the twenty-fourth holder of that office. Unless the worst happens, there will be many, many more.

Hong Kong is administered by the Governor, assisted by an Executive Council of twelve, some of whom are *ex officio* members, and the remainder nominated by the Governor. There is also a Legislative Council of twenty-five, four of them *ex officio*, the others nominated. The procedure in the Legislative Council is based on that of the House of Commons. The duties of both Councils are to advise the Governor, who must consult them, and who can only promulgate laws with the advice and consent of the Legislative Council. There is no pretence at democracy or at representative government. Today, however, there are three Chinese and one Portuguese on the Executive Council and nine Chinese and one Indian on the Legislative Council.

This crown-colonial structure basically dates back to the Colony's foundation. Although set out in simple language, the instructions issued by the Secretary of State to Hong

Kong's first Governor, Sir Henry Pottinger, were, if not disingenuous, at any rate self-contradictory. Hong Kong, he was officially informed, had been occupied 'not with a view to colonization, but for diplomatic, military and commercial purposes'. This conception of a Crown Colony which was not to be colonized seems, to say the least of it, a cloudy one. The theory in Whitehall was that the Hong Kong Governor's first duty was to maintain good relations with the court of Peking, his second to look after the trading interests of British subjects in the Treaty Ports, and only in third place was he to try to set up a constitutional structure within which the new colony and its swarms of immigrants could be governed and kept in order.

Although, as we have seen, Hong Kong was deemed to present peculiar difficulties and to form altogether a special case, the constitution was inevitably devised along conventional crown-colonial lines. The Governor was to consult his Executive Council before taking any action over grants of land, temporary appointments and suspension of public officers. The Legislative Council advised him on law-making, and he could exercise the royal prerogative of pardoning convicted criminals. The British were to be governed under British law, but the Chinese were to be subject to Chinese laws and customs except when these conflicted with what was termed 'those immutable principles of morality which Christians must regard as binding on themselves at all times and in all places'. In this latter provision for the exercise of Chinese law lay the seeds of much corruption, as well as the possibility of future legal chaos.

Both Executive and Legislative Councils were small, and consisted of only three members each, 'high officials' appointed by the Governor. Sir Henry Pottinger, a dictatorial personage, resigned almost immediately after he was appointed in June 1843, and left Hong Kong in May 1844. He was replaced by the scholarly diplomat and sinologue Sir John Davis—'pedantic Sir J. Davies' as the historian Eitel calls him. Davis did enlarge the two Councils by the addition of another two members each, but his efforts to make the constitution acceptable to the Hong Kong merchant body were extraordinarily unsuccessful, and he could not, in Eitel's term, really 'wean' Hong Kong 'amid an amount of tempest and strife which made the impoverished Colonial nursery resound with cries for representative government and with groans condemnatory of monopoly'. Davis was judged by the mercantile community to be even more aloof than Pottinger had been. He was considered offensively erudite and civilized, far too well acquainted with the Chinese language and Chinese history —he had even gone so far as to write a two-volume history of China—and he was given to quoting Latin tags on every possible occasion. As a former servant of the East India Company in South China, he was accused when Governor in Hong Kong of a habit of deference to the Chinese and of disapproving of free trade. When, after four years of squabbling rule, he left the Colony in 1848, the leading newspaper declared that he was 'not only unpopular for his official acts, but unfit for a Colonial Government by his personal demeanour and behaviour'. This newspaper's comments ended, sarcastically, with the Latin exhortation, '*Exi, mi fili, et vide quam minima sapientia mundus hic regitur.*' Even after he had left the island for good, Sir John Davis continued to irritate the business community of Hong

Kong, for when the Anglican colonial church was completed in 1849 it was found that his coat-of-arms, including a bloody hand, was embossed above the porch.

Having signally failed with a military Governor and also with one who was a scholar and sinologist, the Colonial Office now selected a man of what Lord Palmerston called 'practical common sense' as the third viceroy of Hong Kong. This was Sir George Bonham, who had served the Colonial Office for nine years in Australia, Singapore and Malacca and was convinced that 'close attention' to the study of Chinese warped the European mind and destroyed in it all sense of reality. When appointing consuls and vice-consuls to the Treaty Ports Bonham regarded complete ignorance of the Chinese language as a very strong recommendation – even, one suspects, a *sine qua non*. This cavalier attitude to things Chinese endeared him to the British community, as probably did the rumour that the Peking Government had offered a reward for his assassination. Originating amongst the Chinese populace of Hong Kong, this rumour resulted in the novel spectacle of the Governor of a British Crown Colony taking his carriage drives protected by an escort of armed troopers. Though some of the British later asserted that Sir George Bonham was 'a useless governor, purely ornamental, highly decorated and extravagantly paid', he was generally judged to have been 'the first model Governor of Hong Kong' – that is to say the first Governor who kept in personal contact with the merchant community and frequently sought their advice.

With the policy of Sir George Bonham we have, in a sense, the shape of things to come in Hong Kong's social and political life. Pottinger and Davis had successively shut themselves up inside Government House. They had shown no geniality towards the rich and influential traders in opium and salt, tea and silks. Bonham, on the other hand, welcomed such men at Government House and, not long after his installation there, chose fifteen unofficial Justices of the Peace to be his special advisers, thus creating, 'in succession to the merchant princes of former days, an untitled commercial aristocracy'. This was all very well for the fifteen Justices and their families, but it aroused keen resentment amongst the many other wealthy merchants who were not chosen and it laid a solid foundation for that form of social snobbery which, theoretically based on freedom of access to a Governor, has ever been a hallmark of small British colonial communities. Those who were chosen to advise Bonham were called flunkeys and toadies by those who were not; even the favoured fifteen would quarrel amongst themselves over their own precedence at Government House dinner-parties; and the example of a Government House oligarchy and of an untitled commercial aristocracy was imitated in less exalted circles until, socially, the Colony was splintered into 'mutually exclusive cliques and sets'. This process, repeated wherever the British have got together in far-away places with strange-sounding names, was perhaps inevitable; but the chance of forming a genuinely egalitarian and multi-racial community in this brand-new oriental colony was lost within the first six years of British Hong Kong's existence. Nor do such patterns, once set, tend to change. 'Do your daughters marry Hong Kong boys, Mrs X?' I remember artlessly inquiring of my neighbour at a dinner-party in Victoria on my first visit there, seven years ago. 'Oh no, Mr Hen-

nessy, oh no, *no — our daughters fly to London for the season!*'
As I have said, the new Crown Colony was already shaping up. An Anglican church had been built and, when the Bishopric of Victoria was established in 1849, it became the Anglican Cathedral. The Hong Kong Club, scene of many a future cabal against an unpopular or liberal-minded Governor, had come into being with its own exclusive rules. An ice-house was opened by public subscription so that that important ingredient of heavy Victorian meals, the sorbet, could appear on the elaborately laden dinner-tables of the untitled commercial aristocracy as well as on those of what were frankly termed 'the middle orders'. The richer and grander Europeans did not socially recognize those less well-off. The taverns and brothels were full of British soldiers, sailors and seamen and of an element aptly called by Professor Endacott 'the usual off-scourings of the port'. A large Parsee community created their own Parsee graveyard. None of these disparate nationalities, classes, cliques, sets or groups spoke to the others, and certainly not to the Chinese, who were treated as a race of useful sub-humans, were frequently beaten in the streets, and were only allowed out after sundown if they carried a 'lanthorn' and an official pass. The first Bishop of Victoria, the Anglican missionary George Smith, was shocked by the social conditions already pertaining when, in 1849, he arrived in the capital of Hong Kong. He was shocked, too, by the 'moral improprieties and insolent behaviour' of the Europeans, which were arousing the hatred of the Chinese, and by the dire situation of Chinese Christians who expressed to him 'the most impassioned indignation when speaking of the harsh treatment to which they are exposed'.

In spite of the new cathedral there was little, the bishop implied, that was noticeably Christian about the day-to-day behaviour of the British bourgeoisie of Hong Kong.

II

One obvious and inevitable by-product of the carefree and supercilious attitude of Hong Kong Europeans towards the Chinese was a sudden crop or positive harvest of little Eurasians – children, fathered on Chinese girls by foreign businessmen, clerks, seamen, soldiers, sailors and so on. Sir John Bowring, Bonham's successor as Governor of Hong Kong, reported anxiously that these bastards were 'wholly uncared for' and were 'beginning to ripen into a dangerous element out of the dunghill of neglect'. By one of those lurches of policy for which it was known, the Colonial Office had appointed as Bonham's replacement in the governorship a man who disagreed with every single one of his predecessor's basic ideas. Sir John Bowring was an ardent sinologist who believed that the future prosperity of Hong Kong depended on good relations between the European and Chinese communities. Far from sharing Bonham's distrust of any European who spoke Chinese, Bowring thought that most of Hong Kong's difficulties came from the existence of the language barrier. He devised a scheme for British consular cadets to learn Chinese, invented a new European official post, that of 'Protector of the Chinese', and unsuccessfully urged the Secretary of State for the Colonies to agree to an elective element in the Legislative Council, such elected members to be chosen by Chinese as well as British holders of Crown lands. For many years a well-known radical Member of Parliament, and a recognized authority on continental literature, Bowring was a complacent but highly unprejudiced man of the world. He exacerbated the British of Hong Kong, who are said to have abused him more violently than they did any other nineteenth-century Governor of the Colony. The newspapers, which have never, in Hong Kong, achieved any decent journalistic standard, loaded Bowring with 'venomous epithets and libellous accusations'. A correspondent of the *New York Times*, who personally admired him, attributed to Bowring's modest and sensible style of living the unpopularity he aroused in the ostentatious or, as this American journalist put it, 'the detestable' society of Hong Kong.

The appointment of Sir John Bowring to Hong Kong is in itself an example of the enigmatic way in which such posts were then allotted by the Secretary of State for the Colonies. Since there was still no regular or recognized Colonial Service, governorships and lesser positions were handed out to those who applied for them and who had managed to get their names on to 'the Secretary of State's list'. Despite the salary, the prestige, the pomp and the illusion of power that a colonial governorship brought with it, there was no rush of candidates eager to go out and spend five years in charge of a querulous colony in the South China Sea. Bowring had served as British Consul in Canton (where he had learned Chinese) and had then been promoted to Hong Kong. But, like a good many other colonial servants, including my own grandfather, he had originally applied for an overseas post through poverty, having been bankrupted at home. Moreover, the Colonial

Office did not really trust his judgment – Lord John Russell, when Secretary of State, called Bowring 'rather wild upon all subjects' – and he was known for being difficult with his subordinates. In fact, with all his erudition and his good intentions, Bowring was not an ideal governor for Hong Kong.

This matter of the haphazard method of selecting British colonial governors raises the question of how much influence such mid-Victorian pro-consuls ever really had. It might be thought that, in those days of leisurely communications, when neither the Suez Canal nor the submarine telegraph cable existed, the governor of so remote a colony as Hong Kong would have complete power to mould it to his will. Yet, owing in part to the almost automatic hostility of the British merchant community, no early Governor of Hong Kong managed to get much done. The Colony's first historian, the German Dr Eitel, who published in 1895 a massive volume on the reigns of the first eight Governors of Hong Kong, asserts that it was 'remarkable how little really depended upon the character, wisdom or energy of any of these exalted individuals'. To Dr Eitel these first governors seemed to have been little more than eccentric puppets, spaciously installed in Government House but in reality as impotent there as the Heian Emperors in their palaces in medieval Kyoto. His researches had convinced him that each governor was 'possessed of his own idiosyncrasies' and was totally 'controlled by an ever shifting series of Secretaries of State for the Colonies'. But, sceptical about the values and even about the intentions of the governors whose terms he chronicled, Eitel himself cherished a sentimental private myth. This was that, behind the figure-heads in Government House, behind the inconsistencies of Secretaries of State, there loomed 'the ideal but none the less real entity, the genius of British public opinion which inspires and over-rules them all'. To this interesting view of the British Empire Eitel added the yet stranger theory that the British trade presence in Hong Kong and at the Treaty Ports was, in the course of time, plainly destined to 'civilize' China and, afterwards, the remainder of the Far East.

III

To transient visitors in mid-Victorian Hong Kong signs of this civilizing process were not always apparent. They reported that you could not walk up and down the shady, sloping streets of the capital without passing Europeans engaged in belabouring Chinese coolies with sticks and with umbrellas. In 1877 Lord Ronald Gower, a man of great humanity, was deeply shocked by the supercilious attitude to orientals of the young officers of the 74th Regiment, then stationed in the Colony. These youths, who had seemed such charming company when he had met them at the Hong Kong Club, treated all orientals 'as if they were a very inferior kind of animal to themselves'. 'No wonder', Lord Ronald reflected in his diary, 'that we English are so cordially disliked wherever we go. There is nothing more insolent to a foreigner than an English civilian, unless it be a military Englishman.' Pained by these soldiers' boorish arrogance, he refused to tour Japan with a group of them who were going there on leave.

In fairness to these long-dead Europeans, however, we

must not forget that the very high Chinese crime rate of old Hong Kong inspired a genuine sense of fear. The local newspapers of the period were filled with accounts of burglaries and murders. The general atmosphere was one of distrust and panic. The language barrier, and the inability of many English people to distinguish Chinese faces one from another, made things worse. Even progressive developments in the Colony seemed to bring with them some new unforeseen danger. When, in the early eighteen sixties, American river-steamers established a daily run between Canton and Hong Kong, taking Chinese passengers from the mainland at twenty cents a head, it was found that these cheap fares encouraged 'Chinese ruffians', attracted by what were rumoured to be the comparatively humane penal laws of the Colony, to swarm in. Then the great storm-water drains, in themselves feats of engineering and essential to the capital in the rainy season, began to be used by robbers. Known as 'drain-gangs', these groups would creep along these great dark conduits, and then tunnel through and undermine the vaults of banks, the stores of jewellers and the godowns of the bigger merchants. In this way, for instance, in February 1865, the vaults of the Central Bank of Western India were broken into and thousands of dollars' worth of notes taken, together with eleven thousand pounds in gold ingots. Some of these were found strewn about the streets the following morning. Enterprising crimes such as these aroused alarm and fury amongst the Europeans and the richer Chinese of Hong Kong. Flogging, and branding on the neck, were swiftly introduced to make 'Hong Kong and its humane gaol less attractive and comfortable for the gaol birds of Canton'. The fact that these brutal methods did not prove deterrent increased the general sense of insecurity. The Chinese people's automatic hostility to foreigners, which had first been demonstrated during the three-hundred-year Portuguese occupation of Macao, naturally spread to the youthful Colony of Hong Kong, where hatred begat hatred and fear begat fear. And so the vicious circle whirled and spun, some years less dizzily than others, but always in perpetual motion. A peak moment of horror for the European community was reached in January 1857, when a dashing attempt was made to wipe out the whole British community at one fell swoop. This episode occurred during the governorship of Sir John Bowring, who was busy privately conducting an unsuccessful running duel with Yeh, the Chinese Viceroy at Canton. The origin of these hostilities, which finally ended in war and in the Anglo-French occupation of Canton, lay in the seizure by the Cantonese authorities in October 1856 of the lorcha *Arrow*, a Chinese-owned clipper-built ship registered under the British flag. Bowring ordered the naval bombardment of Canton, but when this proved entirely inconclusive, the British Admiral withdrew again to Hong Kong, causing panic amongst the British and Chinese merchants. Protest meetings of merchants criticizing the inefficiency of the Government were held—prototypes for similar gatherings which ever afterwards have punctuated the querulous history of the Colony. The local newspapers began to publish 'a daily chronicle of Chinese atrocities'. In the first fortnight of January 1857 these lists included the shooting of four men 'with fire-balls upon them'; the drugging of three Europeans by doctored soup; a headless body in the Wongnaichung valley; the capture of a British vessel by Chinese soldiers who murdered eleven Europeans and burned the ship; and arson in matsheds* in Queen's Road Central. Life began to seem increasingly precarious and the great firm of Jardine Matheson demanded a naval detachment to guard their premises. In Canton the Chinese viceroy increased the price he had put on European heads and arranged to have the streets of Hong Kong plastered with appeals to the Chinese populace 'to avenge his wrongs by any means whatever', a process repeated in the riots of 1967 when the main public buildings of Hong Kong were found each morning to be decorated with Maoist propaganda printed on rose-pink paper. The British community felt threatened – and helpless.

One of the first prerequisites of normal life the Victorians introduced into their colonial territories was the English breakfast, a meal comprising sausages, fried eggs and bacon, kippers, finnan-haddy and strong tea. Totally unsuited to a tropical climate, the English breakfast remains, in fact, one of the last vestiges of British rule in liberated territories today. It is still to be found bubbling and seething on the stoves of a thousand Government rest-houses and 'Progress Hotels' from Bumpe to Bolgatanga to Onitsha, from Ipoh to Kelantan to Alor Star. It is prevalent throughout the emerald valleys of Mauritius and even in the swamps of Borneo. As essential as the chota-peg at sundown, this ritual British meal naturally reigned in full force in Hong Kong. Like the club-house and the Anglican cathedral, the routine of the heavy English breakfast gave its participants a sense of false stability, and an illusion of being back in

* Large, flimsy structures consisting of bamboo scaffolding and straw matting, and usually open on one side.

Peckham or Devizes. Although cooked by trousered amahs and served by deftly treading Chinese boys, breakfast was clearly the safest of meals, no matter how many atrocities the newspapers revealed as you were eating it. Who would ever expect to be poisoned at an English breakfast? Drugged soup at dusk in some questionable Chinese restaurant, yes; poison at the polished mahogany breakfast-table, no. Yet this is exactly what happened to four hundred Europeans eating breakfast in Hong Kong on the morning of January 15th, 1857.

It would seem to have been generally conceded by the European housewives of Hong Kong that the best quality of bread was that made by the E-sing bakery, which was situated in the Wanchai district and belonged to a Heung-shan man named Cheong Ah-Lum. Imagine, then, the shock that January morning when 'at every European breakfast table there arose the simultaneous cry of "poison in the bread".' When they were later sent home to be analysed at Woolwich, both white and brown loaves were found to contain considerable quantities of arsenic. Lady Bowring, the Governor's wife, became delirious and was forced to withdraw to England where she died. Although no deaths were directly attributed to the 1857 arsenic plot, many people believed their health to have been permanently undermined and 'all received a severe nervous shock by the sudden consciousness of being surrounded by assassins.' European doctors, themselves in pain, scurried about Victoria, and, we are told, 'emetics were in urgent request in every family.'

This effort at mass-murder was believed to have been instigated by the mandarins of Canton, as part of their war of nerves over the *Arrow* incident. Owing to the over-enthusiasm of Cheong Ah-Lum's employees, who had scattered arsenic wholesale in the yeast, the poison had been quickly detected and its effects neutralized. All the same the European community was outraged and demanded that the suspects be immediately executed without trial. Cheong Ah-Lum happened to have crossed over to Macao that very morning. Brought back, he was acquitted by a British jury on lack of evidence. Fifty-two of his men were, however, locked into a fifteen-foot-square room at a police-station—the Government gaol being, as usual, full—and while ten of these were brought to trial, the rest were kept cooped up in the Black Hole of Hong Kong for nearly three weeks until moved on medical advice. When news of the harsh treatment of these suspects was published in London newspapers, the British Government demanded an inquiry. Mass arrests of Chinese vagrants resulted in the deportation of many of them from the Colony, while thousands of others voluntarily emigrated to San Francisco and Australia. We may fancy that for some weeks British families approached the breakfast-table gingerly, but in time the incident became a memory—one more unpleasant memory in the history of inter-community relations in Hong Kong.

IV

The third war with China, originating in the incident of the lorcha *Arrow* and ending in the Treaty of Tientsin, brought British Hong Kong one extremely solid benefit—the cession in perpetuity of the Kowloon Peninsula, which lies three-quarters of a mile across the harbour from Hong

Kong, as well as of Stonecutter's Island. At a solemn public ceremony in January 1861 Kowloon was handed over to the Queen's representative, Lord Elgin, the diplomat who had negotiated the Treaty of Tientsin in 1858. The terms of this treaty, which was intended to conclude the war, having been broken by the Emperor, Lord Elgin had returned to China with a second military force, occupied Peking, and made his personal contribution to the British programme for civilizing the Orient by ordering his soldiery to put the Summer Palace to the sack and to destroy its works of art. He then negotiated a new Treaty, the Peking Convention, one clause of which gave Britain permanent possession of Kowloon. Queen Victoria had now not only 'got' Hong Kong but a portion of the mainland of the Chinese Empire as well.

Before a large audience of Hong Kong residents, and protected by two thousand British troops, Lord Elgin accepted from one of the Canton mandarins a piece of paper containing soil which symbolized the cession of the land. The royal standard was hoisted. Lusty British cheers rang out over the harbour. The men-of-war fired thunderous salutes, and a British battery on Stonecutter's Island joined in. Two days after the ceremony Lord Elgin, who had always loathed Hong Kong and its inhabitants, left the island for Manila 'with unfeigned relief'.

The next question facing Whitehall and the Hong Kong Government was the one which usually followed on all British colonial accretions in the nineteenth century, whether they were the Gambia or Singapore or Labuan: what precisely to do with this latest jewel in the British crown? In the case of Kowloon this problem resolved itself into a fierce and four-year tussle between the colonial Government and the local military authorities. The military insisted that the new territory should be handed over to them, to be used exclusively as a cantonment and a place for army manoeuvres. Backed up by the War Office they declared that the very idea of getting hold of Kowloon in the first place had been the brainchild of the local General, Sir Hope Grant, and that it had always been assumed that the whole object of it was to give the troops airy barracks in a region far healthier than Hong Kong Island. Sir John Bowring had by now left the Colony, lamented only by the Chinese community. His successor, Sir Hercules Robinson, was a far abler administrator and a man immensely popular with the Hong Kong British. Robinson sensibly wanted to use Kowloon to increase the dock-space of the Colony, to build hospitals and private houses on it. He also thought that this strip of land with the mountains at its back would be ideal 'for air and exercise'. Moreover, he felt Kowloon to be 'indispensable to the welfare of the Colony, it being required to keep the Chinese population at some distance and to preserve the European and American community from the injury and inconvenience of intermixture with the Chinese residents'. This *apartheid* mentality appealed strongly to the European residents, still seething with indignation over the arsenic breakfast, and does a good deal to explain the high esteem in which they held Governor Robinson. In the end it was the War Office that won. All the best land in Kowloon was handed over to the redcoats, the remaining parts being divided between the Navy and the colonial Government. The interests of Imperial Defence had prevailed.

V

One of the most efficient services in modern Hong Kong is provided by the ferries which shuttle thousands back and forth from 'Hong Kong-side' to 'Kowloon-side'. They leave the shore at sharp intervals, there is no hanging about, and the brief journey becomes for many of the passengers an almost social occasion as they chatter with their friends and acquaintances and exchange those laughing salutations which make life in even the most impoverished Chinese community seem gay and amiable. Towards nightfall, and later, these throngs of Chinese are peppered with European or American couples, bound for the screeching night-life of Kowloon or simply, in the case of the Americans, for the security of the great Peninsula Hotel which, like the Hilton and the Mandarin on Hong Kong-side, provides that perfect reproduction of the American way of hotel life which seems essential to most Americans abroad.

Stepping off the ferry at Kowloon, one finds it impossible to connect this squawking oriental version of a British midlands city with the territory taken over by Lord Elgin in 1861, and subsequently made into a military cantonment. What was once a pastoral Chinese landscape like one on some muted water-colour scroll, with a small and ageless walled city and a tiny Chinese fort, is now a sprawling, shapeless grey complex of tenements, slums and brightly lit but uninspiring bars. On the asphalt of the terminal double-decker buses wait to be invaded by the jostling crowd, and long taxi-queues form up as though at Waterloo Station. None the less, one's first two or three nights out on Kowloon-side do seem fascinating, and do relieve the claustrophobia engendered by too long a stay upon Hong Kong Island. But this night scene soon palls; and by day you come only to register the monotony and dreary street-planning of Kowloon. Since most of the Colony's factories are situated there, and the living as well as the working conditions are, if possible, worse than those of Hong Kong itself, it is in Kowloon that the most dangerous riots flare up and spread across, by ferry, to the island. It was in a factory with the Firbankian name of 'The Artificial Flower Factory' that the 1967 riots were fomented – riots not of a specifically political nature, but caused by living conditions which have to be seen to be believed, and by rates of pay and working hours which would surely make the great Lord Shaftesbury turn in his grave. Although the rehousing schemes on the outskirts of Kowloon and upon the hills behind it represent an energetic Government effort, the real poverty and squalor of Kowloon are desperate. These are facts that a visitor must find out by a species of private field research. Those well-to-do Europeans and Chinese whose sole interest in life is making money become vague and evasive when you inquire about Hong Kong poverty. You are conducted round model glass and carpet and toy factories. The rest you must find out for yourself.

I realized this on New Year's Eve, 1959, when on my second evening in Hong Kong I was kindly invited to a dinner-party which took place in a penthouse apartment belonging to the managing director of a famous old British firm. It was the same entertainment at which I met the lady who sent her daughters to London 'for the season'. In the course of this meal I made some ingenuous inquiries of a Chinese gentleman at my table as to how and where I could see the 'rooftop people' – Chinese families who, I had been given to understand, lived in shacks and cardboard boxes on the tops of tenement buildings in Victoria. Although there are still to this day some seventy to eighty thousand of these elevated squatters in Hong Kong, my new friend smilingly replied that he had never heard of anybody in Hong Kong living on a rooftop, and that if they did so it was probably by preference. The next few nights, therefore, I devoted to a personal exploration of the rooftop population, and also of the alleys in Wanchai where families were sleeping on tiered bunks in the rain. These visits did much to modify the romantic ideas about Hong Kong which I had brought with me to that colony – ideas founded on the reading of Victorian travellers' tales, and on research into the life of my grandfather, Sir John Pope Hennessy, the first Governor to initiate a liberal policy towards the Hong Kong Chinese.

4

VICTORIAN VICTORIA

I

ONCE the British administration was well established, Hong Kong began to change its aspect and ceased to be the desolate, scrub-covered rock which had aroused Prince Albert's mirth. The very earliest British settlement at Queen's Town (soon renamed Victoria) consisted of a huddle of godowns, shacks and tents along that portion of the harbour shore still known as Happy Valley. Despite lethal malarial fevers and a series of destructive typhoons, this settlement flourished. Within a twelvemonth of its foundation the town was sheltering some fifteen thousand people, including small detachments of British and Indian troops; the shacks and palm-leafed hutments were being replaced by wooden houses shipped from Singapore, as well as by a handful of imposing granite or brick-and-granite buildings. In the next three decades elegant examples of nineteenth-century colonial architecture—houses, halls, administrative offices, churches—were added, and Victoria swiftly became a solid-looking, prosperous, overcrowded tropical city spread out along the islands' northern shore and clambering in steep terraces up the hillsides at the back.

That speed which seems the keynote to Hong Kong's

commercial life was already at work. Less than forty years after its foundation an English visitor could describe Victoria as 'magnificent':

> The English and Romish cathedrals, the Episcopal Palace, with St Paul's College, great high blocks of commercial buildings, huge sugar factories, great barracks in terraces, battery above battery, Government House and massive stone wharves ... and over all, its rich folds spread out fully on the breeze, floated the English flag.

This same observer, the inveterate globe-trotter Miss Isabella Bird who visited Hong Kong in 1878, compared the 'very beautiful city' of Victoria to Genoa – a comparison which seems startling indeed today.

> It reminds me [wrote Miss Bird in a letter to her sister] of Genoa but that most of its streets are so steep as to be impassable for wheeled vehicles, and some are merely grand flights of stairs, arched over by dense foliaged trees, so as to look like some tropical, coloured, deep colonnades. It has covered green balconies with festoons of creepers, lofty houses, streets narrow enough to exclude much of the sun, people and costumes of all nations, processions of Portuguese priests and nuns; all its many-coloured life is seen to full advantage under this blue sky and brilliant sun.

Another English visitor, who was in Hong Kong in the same year as Miss Bird, called Victoria 'this marvellously picturesque place', which evoked his childhood's notions of the Arabian Nights.

> I found myself [wrote this particular traveller, the sculptor Lord Ronald Gower] transported two thousand years back in ancient Rome or glorious Carthage. This illusion is helped no doubt by the coloured dresses and graceful drapery of the Chinese, and by the somewhat classical style of the white houses, with their porticoes and colonnades and balconies sparkling under the intensely brilliant sunshine, outlined sharply against the almost purple sky.

Here we have two contemporary travellers in the latter half of the nineteenth century who, while reacting rather differently to the visual impact of Hong Kong (to one it seemed a Genoa beneath a sky of blue, to the other a city built by the ancient Romans under a purple sky), were both at one upon a cardinal point: the extraordinary beauty of the capital of Hong Kong Island at that time.

Amongst the varied pitfalls of travel-writing is the temptation to describe one place in terms of another. It is into this trap that Miss Isabella Bird tumbles when she likens old Hong Kong's dappled streets to those of the Mediterranean port of Genoa. The steep, stepped wynds of Hong Kong, which, in the old quarter of the town, run uphill like stone ladders, are in my own experience unique, and surely can never have resembled the Genoese *vicoli*.

Another nineteenth-century writer on Hong Kong, a Governor of the Colony whose name was Sir William des Voeux, found as he looked down from Mountain Lodge, his official bungalow on the Peak, that the town of Victoria spread out far below reminded him of a certain view of

Naples: 'the sharp lines of the streets, with the densely packed houses on either side, giving the idea of roads cut deep into solid rock, and reminding me much of a similar sight which may be seen from a hill of much less height above Naples'. Sir William and Miss Bird were aiming at explanation rather than evocation, at conveying to readers who had never seen Hong Kong what the city might be like, at interpreting, therefore, the alien in terms of the more familiar. Lord Ronald Gower, an artist keeping a journal, extracts from which he later published, realized, on the other hand, that what he was seeing in Hong Kong was utterly unlike anything he had ever seen before; and his hazy, excited vision of the nineteenth-century Crown Colony as recalling his childhood fantasies about Assyria and ancient Rome seems to me to give a clearer impression of the bewildering, highly coloured life of old Hong Kong than all the analogies with Italian ports and harbours put together.

II

There were, however, visitors to whom the capital of nineteenth-century Hong Kong did not seem in the least Italian. It seemed overwhelmingly British, and reminded them of Gibraltar. In her best-selling *A Voyage in the 'Sunbeam'*, a lively journal of a trip round the world with her husband and family in their yacht, young Mrs Thomas Brassey wrote of a first stroll through Victoria in the winter of 1877:

> Soldiers and sailors abound in the streets; and if it were not for the sedan-chairs and palanquins, in which every-body is carried about by Chinese coolies with enormous

hats, one might easily fancy oneself at dear old Gib., so much do these dependencies of the Crown in foreign countries resemble one another, even in such opposite quarters of the globe.

A born romantic, who headed her chapter on Hong Kong with the quotation

> Sails of silk and ropes of sandal
> Such as gleam in ancient lore,
> And the singing of the sailors,
> And the answer from the shore,

Mrs Brassey was also a sharp and practical observer. After tiffin at the Hong Kong Hotel she noted that this hostelry was not 'a very desirable abode, being large, dirty, and ill kept. At one o'clock a bell rang, and the visitors all rushed in and took their places at various little tables, and were served with a "scrambly" sort of a meal by Chinese boys.' She thought the town itself European in style, with wide and handsome streets, stone buildings, deep verandas and arcades. The hillside to which the town clung was at that time broken up into 'ferny, moss-covered banks, overhung by tropical trees, close to some of the principal offices'. On the other hand the Chinese part of the town, standing 'quite away from the foreign settlement', was dirty and crowded, for all its broad streets and large painted houses, gay with the daubed ideographs of their proprietors' names and of advertisements of the goods they sold. In the Chinese quarter Mrs Brassey's pocket was picked of a one-dollar note, which was retrieved by her escorts who, after giving the thief 'a good shaking', let him go.

Like other tourists, the Brasseys were dismayed by that curse of old Hong Kong, the perpetual use of pidgin English. They heard English merchants giving their clerks and compradors important orders in 'the silliest of baby-talk'. 'Take the lady's bag upstairs', for instance, became 'Take piecey missisy one piecy bag topside'. Their English acquaintances explained that this complex gibberish was 'easier to a Chinaman's intellect'. A contemporaneous visitor wrote of pidgin English as 'revolting': 'The most dignified persons demean themselves by speaking it. How the whole English-speaking community, without distinction of rank, has come to communicate with the Chinese in this baby-talk is extraordinary.'

The Brasseys' visit had coincided with the last day of the races, a popular annual event at which segregation was only practised inside the grandstand, which had a thatched roof, verandas and sun-blinds, and contained 'the most luxurious basket chairs one could possibly desire'. There were also private stands and tiffin rooms. The attendance was very large, many of the spectators having come over from Macao or down from Canton and Shanghai. The horses were some of them Australian, but most were little Chinese ponies with European riders whose legs almost touched the ground. The proceedings ended with a European ball in the town.

III

It will now have been gathered that by the time of the visits of the Brasseys, Miss Isabella Bird and Lord Ronald Gower, the social life of European Hong Kong was far advanced.

The daily round was well established and could even have been called sophisticated; and however much they might dislike seeing Chinese beaten in the city streets, or deride the use of pidgin English, there was one fact upon which all Victorian tourists were in agreement—the warm and expansive hospitality which the European community hastened to extend to distinguished visitors. Long past were the days when Hong Kong was regarded as a dubious asset. Now, with its fine wharves, its public buildings and its private mansions, its harbour crowded with the merchant shipping of the world, it was recognized, in the words of one of Queen Victoria's grandsons, as 'a little England in the eastern seas, the creation of British energy, enterprise and industry'. For distinguished travellers in the East, a visit to Hong Kong had become a vital part of their itinerary. In April 1879, for example, the bibulous former President of the United States, General Ulysses S. Grant, who was trundling round the world with his suite, was 'magnificently' entertained at Government House, while later in the same year Prince Thomas of Savoy, the Duke of Genoa, arrived on board a frigate of the Italian navy.

In 1880, to the excitement of the British community, the Colony was visited by the first member of Queen Victoria's family to set foot on the island. This was the eighteen-year-old Prince Henry of Prussia, the brother of the future Kaiser Wilhelm II. Although a German prince, Prince Henry was none the less the grandson of the Queen-Empress, and his visit aroused pleasurable anticipation. But it was found that Prince Henry, who was an officer on the *Prinz Adalbert*, and stayed with his equerry Baron von Seckendorff at Government House, disappointingly wished to be treated as a simple naval officer and regarded his visit to Hong Kong as a species of private holiday on shore.

> He seems to enjoy his holiday and quiet life on shore, playing lawn tennis with my wife and myself, driving her Sumatra ponies and walking about incognito with Baron Seckendorff [the Governor, Sir John Pope Hennessy, wrote to the Marchioness of Ely, Queen Victoria's principal lady-in-waiting]. He says it is the first time he has tasted fresh butter since leaving Europe. Fortunately it is the coolest month of May we have had here for years, but I have begged of him to avoid going out in the middle of the day, and never to do so, when the sun is shining, without his sun-helmet and an umbrella ... He plays lawn tennis with real vigour, in fact he strikes the ball too hard though we have a very long court. At billiards, too, and driving the Deli ponies he never gets tired ... Everyone speaks in admiration of his sweet expression, his bright blue eyes and pleasant voice.

This letter was given, as was intended, to the Queen. The only opportunities which the 'principal people of Hong Kong' had of meeting Prince Henry was at the Queen's Birthday dinner, and at a State lunch-party at Government House, when the Governor unveiled a portrait of the Prince Consort and the Prince said a few words about his grandmother the Queen. In the following year, however, the prospect of another royal visit aroused a fresh flutter of hope amongst the ladies and gentlemen of Hong Kong society. This was the news that Admiral Lord Clanwilliam's Detached Squadron would be dropping anchor there shortly before Christmas. Amongst the Detached Squadron was H.M.S. *Bacchante*, aboard which, as everyone knew, were the Prince of Wales's two sons – the heir-presumptive to the throne, Prince Albert Victor of Wales, and his younger brother Prince George, afterwards King George V. Prince Albert Victor, known as Prince Eddy, was eighteen and his brother one year younger. They were spending three years at sea, as part of an unusual educational programme which had been devised by the Prince of Wales and initially resisted by Queen Victoria. The youths were accompanied by their tutor Mr Dalton, whose charge it was to continue, on shipboard, the lethargic Prince Eddy's patchy education, and by their valet Fuller. They were treated as ordinary midshipmen, trained and took examinations with their shipmates and were only accorded royal honours in countries which insisted on it, such as Egypt and Japan.

The arrival of H.M.S. *Bacchante* in Hong Kong coincided with the midshipmen's written examinations, and Lord Clanwilliam was quite rightly not prepared to release the Princes from their work so that they could be lionized by the British of Hong Kong. Very strict instructions had been issued to the Governor on this point, and Lord Clanwilliam was amazed on reaching the Colony to find that everyone from the Governor downwards had disregarded them. A great ball was to be given at Government House, another by public subscription in the town. The whole of Victoria was illuminated, there were to be a regatta and a Chinese dragon procession, and interminable salutes booming out over the harbour. Lord Clanwilliam went personally to protest to the Governor, only to be informed by Sir John

Sir John Pope Hennessy, K.C.M.G., Governor of Hong Kong, 1877–82

(*above*) The city and harbour of Victoria, Hong Kong, in 1898

(*left*) Sir Frederick (later Lord) Lugard, Governor of Hong Kong, 1907–12 and founder of the University there

(*right*) Main block of the University of Hong Kong, 1960. The buildings stand on a steep hillside overlooking the harbour

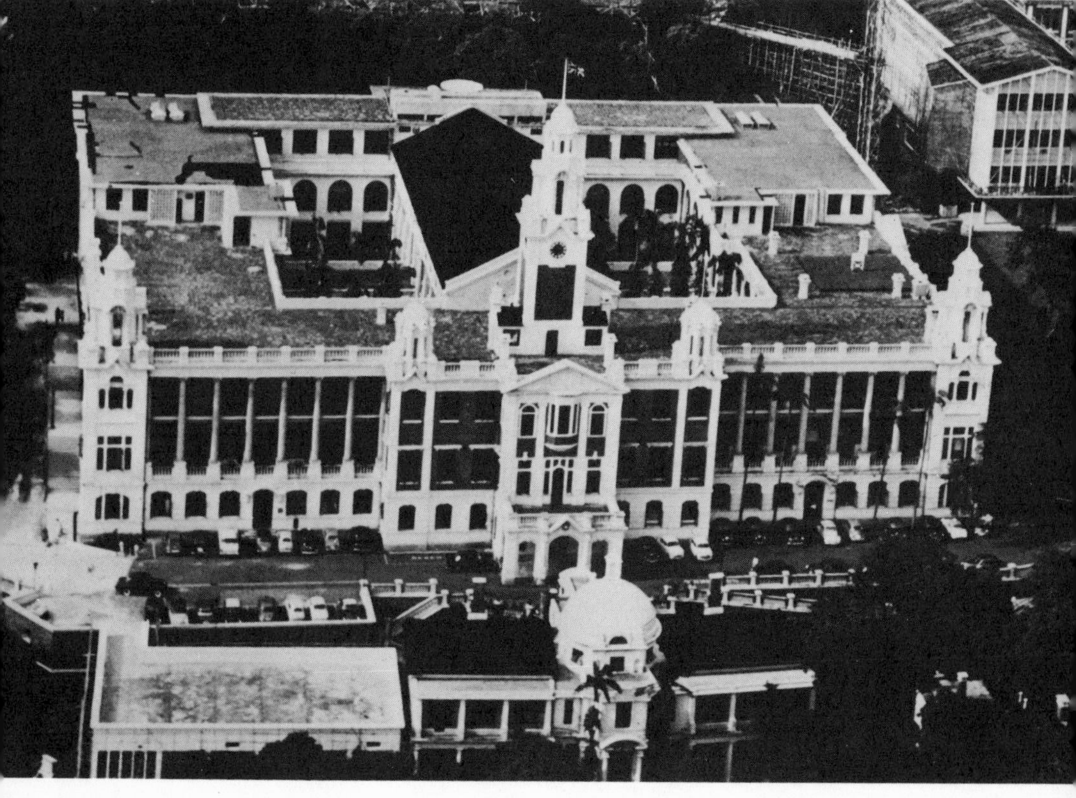

(*left*) British official life in Hong Kong: scene at a Government House garden party, 1956

(*below*) A typical street scene in modern Kowloon. Money changers abound throughout Kowloon and Victoria

Pope Hennessy that he had 'received special commands of Her Majesty which would over-ride Lord Clanwilliam's instructions'. Lord Clanwilliam, in his report home, added that the Governor had taken 'no steps to make public the Princes' actual position in the Squadron, but on the other hand encouraged preparations on a large scale for their entertainment.' In London the Colonial Office, who were accustomed to, and long exasperated by, Pope Hennessy's high-handed behaviour were sceptical of the existence of special instructions from the Queen. Later they were rendered furious when they received a bill for £800 for photographs of the Princes' visit. In his reply the Governor admitted that the bill was 'apparently rather large' but added that every five years or so it was valuable to have photographs taken to show how the tree-planting was getting on. This total *non sequitur* did not mollify the officials in Downing Street, who rated this royal photographic spree 'a monstrous piece of extravagance'. Over the entertaining, Lord Clanwilliam won the day, and the only official appearances of the Princes were at the regatta and at the public subscription ball in the city buildings, both events taking place after the midshipmen's examinations were over.

In the year 1886, Macmillans published a vast work in two volumes, *The Cruise of Her Majesty's Ship 'Bacchante'*, dedicated to the Queen by its joint 'authors', Prince Eddy and Prince George. In fact this pedestrian book, which runs to fourteen hundred pages, was compiled by their tutor Mr Dalton; it was full of classical allusions and statistics and of detailed but somewhat tepid descriptions of what the two Princes had done and seen. Predictably the Hong Kong section opens: 'Hong Kong reminds us at first sight of Gibraltar, but it is not very like, except that it is a lofty hill with a town at foot and ships in front.' Like other visitors they found the streets of Victoria 'wide and clean, full of chairs with green canopies and wickerwork sides, on long bamboo carrying poles, and of jin-rickshaws'.

They preferred the motion of the rickshaws, which had only recently been introduced into Hong Kong in any quantity. The Princes were also under the mistaken impression that there were no wheeled carriages in Hong Kong.

On the Praya, by the water's edge, the Princes were shown one of the sights of old Hong Kong: the unloading of Indian opium, in large square packets weighing a hundredweight each and worth, when the crude drug had been prepared, £140 a packet. They were told that two or three thousand chests arrived a week and that one hundred thousand such chests went over to the Chinese mainland annually. The trade seemed to be chiefly in the hands of Parsees, who wore high, stiff black hats, and one of whom then held the monopoly for selling and preparing opium, for which he paid the Hong Kong Government £40,000 a year. The opium trade was spiralling and was still the pride of many of the merchants of Hong Kong.

To visitors of this period the Crown Colony, which by then had a population of some hundred and sixty thousand souls, must clearly have seemed to form a charming, welcoming and diverting caravanserai, a British creation, moreover, and so a natural subject for any patriot's approval. This old Hong Kong has vanished—the Hong Kong of scarlet-curtained palanquins swaying on their sturdy bearers' shoulders, of mandarins with pigtails and jade hat-buttons and robes of startling satins encrusted with gold thread, of white porticoes and balconies shaded by yellow jasmine and by flame-trees, of an oriental silken hustle in the streets, of a silence shattered only by the hoarse cry of the rickshaw boys plying for hire or of the sampan girls quarrelling on the water-front. All this today is gone like smoke. Many of the old merchants' houses still linger on in the more down-at-heel areas of the city, but their beauty is now only the beauty of rot, nostalgia and decay.

It is relevant at this point to consider the second Hong Kong, which transient visitors like the Wales Princes or Mrs Brassey only glimpsed if they wandered in the Chinese market or watched a dragon procession on Confucius's birthday. This was a purely Chinese city, built at some distance from the British part of Victoria, and which made the capital, in an ethnic sense, not one city but two. For, until the arrival of the liberal-minded Governor Pope Hennessy, no persons of Chinese birth were permitted to buy land, to build, or to live in the European quarter of the town. An enemy to every form of racial segregation, my grandfather not only authorized but encouraged the Chinese to move into the hitherto exclusively European area of Victoria. For this wise and humane action he earned the deathless hatred of the British merchant community and the fond loyalty of the Chinese.

5

THE COMMUNAL CHASM

I

DURING the stay of Queen Victoria's grandson, Prince Henry of Prussia, at Government House in 1880, there occurred a characteristic squabble between Governor Hennessy and General Donovan, who commanded the Hong Kong garrison. Trivial in itself, this row is entirely significant of the racial stresses to which the Colony was subject. It was a tradition that at the Queen's Birthday dinner, on May 26th, the garrison band should be detailed to play at Government House. In May 1880 General Donovan point-blank refused to release the band, and even arranged an alternative Queen's Birthday dinner at the barracks. The incident was solved by reference to London, where it was decided that the band must naturally play at Government House. But behind this undignified episode lay the General's detestation of the Governor, with whom he was no longer on speaking terms. His prejudice arose from the fact that Governor Hennessy had recently issued an ordinance permitting respectable Chinese to buy and build houses on land near the barracks, in what had always been regarded as an integral part of the European quarter of the town. The General was convinced that the proximity of any Chinese households to the British barracks and the officers' quarters could only prove demeaning and unhealthy.

It will be recalled that one of the objects of Governor Robinson in claiming land at Kowloon for civilian use was that of preserving 'the European and American community from the injury and inconvenience of intermixture with the Chinese residents' near the European quarter of Victoria. This attitude to the race upon which they were battening was endemic to the British community. Another of my grandfather's persistent attacks on this prejudice involved him in a bitter quarrel with Mr Keswick, of the firm of Jardine Matheson. This storm centred round the admission of Chinese to the Hong Kong Museum, of which Mr Keswick was chairman. The museum had a small annual Government grant, and was in the main financially supported by the British traders but also by the rate-paying Chinese. Pope Hennessy discovered that the Chinese were permitted into the museum and library only in the mornings and that, after the lunch-time closure for cleaning, the premises were exclusively reserved for Europeans and non-Chinese. The Keswick faction argued that the Chinese tended to use the museum too much, and that their presence there was unsavoury; whereupon the Governor cut off the Government grant. Back in the Colonial Office in London his attitude was supported in a qualified manner—'A little tact might usefully have replaced these impassioned harangues, but of course no class distinctions can be tolerated in a building even in part supported by public money'—and

Lord Kimberley, then Secretary of State, commented that 'garlic-eating ratepayers must be endured by those who use their money'. The basic principles of British imperial policy as expressed in London were usually more just and temperate than those of the colonials themselves. But it was with the colonials that the Chinese had to live.

The principles of social segregation, practised at Hong Kong on the highest levels, were summed up by a contemporary: 'European merchants have ever been the leaders and the Chinese merchants the indispensable hangers-on and go-betweens of the China Trade.' You did not ask hangers-on and go-betweens, however indispensable, to dine at your house, and when first Sir Arthur Kennedy, and then his successor Sir John Pope Hennessy, began to receive prominent Chinese at Government House as a matter of course, they were regarded as guilty of subversion. On a lower level, beneath the rich Chinese merchants with whom profitable business could be conducted, the rest of the large Chinese community were distrusted as dishonest, potentially dangerous, malevolent, entangled in mysterious secret societies, foolish in their religious beliefs and only suitable to be clerks, shroffs, amahs, house-boys and coolies. Even the officials in Whitehall, although they were, as I have shown, prepared to give a limited support to the rights of 'subject races', inclined to have doubts about Chinese reliability. When protests began to pour in from Hong Kong against the rise in crime and Pope Hennessy's prison reforms, his abolition of branding for criminals and of flogging in the gaols, his criticism of the night-pass system and his permission for the Chinese to build in Victoria wherever they wished, a leading Colonial

Office adviser briefed the Secretary of State in cautious vein:

> To my mind the history of all this trouble is a simple one. Mr Hennessy observes on arriving that long residence among Chinese, & familiarity with the Chinese character, has led the residents in Hong Kong to believe that a Chinaman is not to be dealt with as an Englishman or even as an Indian or a Malay might be. He thinks this inhuman, and determines to set to work vigorously to reform what he believes to be a grave abuse. But, having no political wisdom, he proceeds in such a manner as to alienate from him all public sympathy and support, & ultimately to cause a sort of panic as to his intentions & their probable results.

So strongly did the Hong Kong traders resent what they called Hennessy's 'Chinese policy' that they and their wives ceased to accept invitations to Government House and when, in March 1882, he left the Colony for good, none of the British business community assembled at the wharf for the conventional leave-taking ceremony. Leading members of the Chinese community, who had sent deputations to call on Sir John at Government House and to present him with gifts and with silken banners embroidered with tributes to his humanity, did, however, attend at the wharf to bid him farewell. These banners are now in my possession, but to me it is even more gratifying to know that, in the pidgin English of the poor and downtrodden Chinese of Hong Kong, he was known as 'Number One Good Friend'.

I have dwelt at some length upon the Hong Kong career

of John Pope Hennessy not because he was my grandfather but because he is now generally recognized as 'the first Governor to be shocked by the unequal treatment of the Chinese'. The words are those of Professor Endacott, who adds: 'He treated the Chinese as partners and largely because of this he was hated by the Europeans. In his enlightened policy he was ahead of his time.' It is only fair to recall that it was Pope Hennessy's immediate predecessor in office, Sir Arthur Kennedy (also an Irishman), who first invited prominent Chinese citizens to Government House receptions; but these were chiefly the compradors or agents of the leading English merchants, and even so Sir Arthur's hospitality aroused the ire of the British traders. Sir Arthur likewise 'for some time encouraged the Chinese to bring any public grievances they might have before him', but before he left the Colony he had changed his mind. The administration of Sir John Pope Hennessy thus forms a watershed in the history of Hong Kong—a thought to ponder over if we reflect that all this earnest Catholic Irishman tried to do in this, as in every other Crown Colony entrusted to him, was to treat the 'native races' as human beings with rights equal to those of the Europeans who regarded themselves as white overlords. As the young Governor of the tiny islet of Labuan, a post he held from 1867 to 1871, Hennessy became almost notorious as a pioneer when he invited Indians, Malays and Chinese to his official entertainments and made personal friends amongst these communities. His Hong Kong activities were but a logical development of these earlier, tentative efforts on a swamp off Borneo.

II

In his attempts to help the Chinese community to equality, Governor Hennessy was greatly aided by Bishop Thimoleon Raimondi, an imposing bearded giant of a man originally from the Milan Mission, who became the First Vicar Apostolic of Hong Kong. By the merchant community Bishop Raimondi was regarded as my grandfather's *éminence grise* and indeed, with his extensive knowledge of the East and of the specific problems of Hong Kong and Kowloon, he was of very great value to the Governor. In a chapter devoted to race relations within the Colony it seems to me vital to direct attention briefly to the influence there of the only power wholly divorced from trade and from officialdom—the Roman Catholic Church. Staffed by Portuguese, Irish and Chinese priests this Church, with its total belief in racial and class equality, has for generations acted as a leaven in the Hong Kong community, where Anglican missionaries so often and so signally failed.

In the early days of the Colony the British community had found it fashionable to support Anglican missionary schools and other attempts to improve, as they deemed it, the Chinese character. It was soon discovered that the educated and richer Chinese preferred to send their sons to China to be educated and were not too interested in St Paul's College, Dr Legge's Anglo-Chinese College or the Morrison Institute. Admirable in themselves, these Establishment institutions did not appeal to the Chinese, and by 1895 St Paul's College, for instance, had not produced 'a single native minister or any official interpreter', while the students of all three Anglican colleges had 'gained at different times an unenviable notoriety in Police Court cases.' These disappointing results led the British merchants to infer that 'an English education, even when conducted on a religious basis, fails to effect any moral reform, and rather tends to draw out the vicious elements inherent in the Chinese character.' Charitable support for the Anglican missionary schools thereupon dwindled, and it was left to the Catholics, who had a seminary for the training of Chinese priests in Victoria, to carry on with their own plans and policies, which did not include on their curricula contempt for or distrust of the Chinese.

Catholicism had come to Hong Kong from the moment of the Crown Colony's inception. In 1841, the year in which the British first occupied the island, the Portuguese settlement of Macao, forty miles away across the mouth of the Pearl River, was still the organizing centre in the East of what I have just called the one international power wholly divorced from trading—the Roman Catholic Church. Macao had for long been the headquarters of the representative of the Congregation for the Propagation of the Faith, an official in charge of all Catholic missions to China, Japan and other countries of the Orient. It also contained an institution very puzzling to most British colonials—a seminary for the training of Chinese-born missionary priests. This Far Eastern branch of the *Propaganda Fide* was currently in the charge of a vigorous and imaginative young Swiss Monsignor, Théodore Joset. It was to Monsignor Joset that a Roman Catholic member of the embryonic Hong Kong administration had appealed, in the first weeks of the new Colony's existence, for the urgent dispatch thither of a Catholic priest.

The urgency was prompted by military considerations. British troops in the temporary barracks at Victoria, and in the sodden, tented camps at Stanley and at Aberdeen, were dying of fever at the rate of four or five a day. As in Kipling's India, there was a large percentage of Irishmen amongst these British troops—lads who, to escape starvation in their own occupied country, had been driven, by the irony of circumstance, to enlist under the colours of the Famine Queen. These Irish youths were dying without the sacraments and with no Roman Catholic chaplain to comfort their last moments. The appeal to Macao was the result.

Monsignor Joset crossed the mouth of the wide Pearl River to Hong Kong and, with a prescience and an optimism which even the British Government in London did not then share, perceived the potential importance of Hong Kong as a major Western outpost in the East. He wrote post-haste to the Vatican, which, for once, acted promptly. By a papal decree of April 1841 Hong Kong Island, and an area six leagues wide round it, were created an ecclesiastical prefecture, with the young Swiss Monsignor as prefect. Welcomed by the Hong Kong authorities, he was asked to select a site for a Catholic church. By this time the scramble for building land was at its height, and all the level spaces, both in the new town and at East Point, were already occupied or bespoken. Joset was therefore obliged to choose a site merely described as 'less precipitous than the rest'. On this lot, which was situated between the Powder Magazine and the Barracks, he constructed a small matshed church, with a hut for the first resident priest, the Spanish Franciscan Father Navarro, beside it. The church was modest in size because Monsignor Joset had been led to believe that the only Catholics in Hong Kong were the Irish soldiery, who clearly could not all be expected to be free of duties at the same time on the same morning. In February 1842 the first Mass was said before 'a good muster of Irish soldiers', who promised that by the following Sunday every Catholic in the Colony would attend. So efficiently did they round up their co-religionists that a week later the little church could not hold one quarter of those wishing to attend Mass. Monsignor Joset at once decided to build a new church to hold a congregation of one thousand persons. The foundation stone was laid in June 1842. At the same time a presbytery, a school and an orphanage were built, and land obtained for a cemetery. The Monsignor's next step was to move the offices of the *Propaganda Fide* from Macao to Hong Kong, as well as the seminary for Chinese students for the priesthood. He himself did not long survive the Hong Kong epidemics, and, dying at the age of thirty-eight, he now lies buried behind the high altar of the Roman Catholic Cathedral in Victoria. Thus began an influence which has ever since been potent in Hong Kong; for, although only some five per cent of the total Chinese population of nearly four millions is Roman Catholic, the educational work of North Italian or Irish or Chinese priests, Canossian Sisters and other Catholic missionaries is everywhere salient in modern Hong Kong. Believers in total racial equality, Roman Catholics did, as I have indicated, do a good deal in nineteenth-century Hong Kong to counteract the ill effects of British prejudice against the Chinese. Relics of this old prejudice are still to be found in modern Hong Kong—as for instance in the rules of that dim, select and staid bastion of Englishry in the East, the Hong Kong Club, which forbids full membership to gentlemen of Chinese birth.

Can one assess the reasons for this old prejudice? And why did it infect not only the colony of Hong Kong but the British merchant societies of the Treaty Ports as well? In Shanghai, for instance, before the First World War, to learn Chinese was to be considered an eccentric, to invite a Chinese to lunch or dine a joke in inconceivably poor taste.

III

Racial prejudice is, as we are all aware, based on fear: a fear of the unfamiliar, the incomprehensible and the alien. In old Hong Kong this fear was obviously enhanced, among the British, by a dramatic incident like the poisoned breakfasts of 1857, by bank robberies and murders. But the Chinese in Hong Kong seemed to possess yet another suspicious characteristic—the apparently enigmatic; and a quality of self-sufficiency which was once called 'clannish exclusiveness'. Rejecting an English education and sending their sons to be educated in Canton, the leaders of the Chinese community further disappointed the English by refusing to wear European clothes or to adopt English ways of living. They took no part in local politics but organized wild-cat strikes of coolies, house-boys and clerks when the Government threatened to pass legislation the leading Chinese disliked. In a sentence remarkable perhaps for its naivety the historian Eitel declared that 'in proportion as the leading Chinese residents learned ... to understand the principles of British communal liberty, there appeared among them a tendency to retire into their own shell, deliberately refusing any identification with the European community.' Where, in fact, it was not unreasonably asked, did their loyalties lie? What would they do in a crisis? Were they to be trusted at all?

These doubts, which could not fail to influence the Hong Kong British, were harboured within the Colonial Office itself. In theory it would be an excellent move to appoint a Chinese to the Legislative Council—'but', wrote a nineteenth-century Secretary of State, 'in the event of difficulties, actual or threatened, between England and China, a Chinese Councillor might be anything but trustworthy; and yet, if permanently appointed, it might be very impolitic to remove him.' The same statesman, Sir Michael Hicks-Beach, reminded the Governor of Hong Kong in another private letter that

> of course our position at Hong Kong with regard to China is a very peculiar one—and demands, I should think, special caution in dealing with a people who, however friendly in appearance or even in reality to their English rulers, yet must surely have sympathies & connections with the Chinese Empire from which much danger might result.

This was, of course, the anomaly and the dilemma of the British Empire in a nutshell—from Africa to the West Indies, from India to Singapore: could you trust the subject races in a crisis? Could you in fact trust a loyalty which was superficial rather than spontaneous, a loyalty imposed upon them from above? In Hong Kong, in Kowloon and still more so in the New Territories* this uncertitude

* The acquisition in 1898, on a ninety-nine-year lease, of the New Territories, 365 square miles of the Chinese mainland behind Kowloon, will be discussed in a subsequent chapter.

was, and probably remains, politically and geographically, acute.

It is my private theory that—apart from the British assumption of an inborn superiority—one of the most fundamental causes of what Eitel called 'the chasm' separating the British and Chinese in old Hong Kong must be sought in the essentially transient quality of the European businessmen and their families. Governors and Government officials by their very nature came and went, but so did the other, mercantile Europeans. When social historians of the Colony, from Eitel onwards, speak of the Hong Kong British as 'residents', the term seems to imply a state of permanence that seldom existed. Even eminent pioneers like William Jardine and Sir James Matheson spent respectively the one only eight years, the other only ten, in setting up their world-famous firm in Canton and then in Macao. Their successors in Hong Kong retired home to Great Britain when they felt like it. Lesser merchants and their families were likewise in the Colony for a term of years merely, and then headed for comfortable houses in Haslemere or Richmond, where only the porcelain, the jade, the lacquer screens and their living-room carpets proved that they had ever been Hong Kong 'residents'. Together with the fact that their whole stint in Hong Kong was dedicated to the swift accumulation of money—with private squabbles, amateur theatricals, balls and race-going thrown in—this ephemeral presence meant that they scarcely had the time, even had they had the inclination, to come to terms with Chinese culture and Chinese beliefs. These seemed to them in any case so alien, so illogical and so perverse that they tended to shrug them off with a laugh or a grimace.

This was particularly apparent in their attitude to two important areas of Chinese practice—the Chinese attitude towards medicine and sanitation, and the Confucian attitude towards death.

In the sphere of sanitation the Chinese quarters of the city were the bane of a succession of sanitation experts, for their inhabitants refused to recognize the benefits of the water-closet as against their own traditional and, in their eyes, completely successful dry-earth system. In medicine they rejected all Western advances save for vaccination, the efficacy of which even their doctors could not deny. The secretive tendency of Chinese doctors in the early days of the Tung Wah Hospital, when the ingredients of remedies were concealed from inquisitive Europeans, aroused intense antipathy. Just as the herbal cures indubitably effected by African witch-doctors used to seem incredible to British residents and medical men, so did the contents of Chinese druggists' shops in Hong Kong appear a suitable subject for mirth. What could you think of a medical system which prescribed rhinoceros skin and rhinoceros horn, tiger bones, dried snake, seahorses, or the water in which monkey or deer bones had been reduced, as remedies for specific ailments and diseases? And when you accidentally discovered that 'the fungus that grows on the inner wood of a coffin, opposite the nose and mouth of a corpse' had also important curative properties, laughter ceased and revulsion set in.

Equally unpleasant and incomprehensible in most British eyes was the conventional Chinese feeling about death. This feeling is the upshot of two distinct principles: that no Chinese man or woman should die in the family house, and that burial can take place only in conditions laid down after mysterious Fung Shui consultations. It was some time before the British authorities grasped the fact that the poorer Chinese were being carried off to die in death-houses and that their corpses were often stored in coffins amongst the moribund. It was only in the late eighteen sixties that the Surveyor-General discovered that the I Ts'z temple, the site for which had been granted to the Chinese as far back as 1851, was being used both as a death-house and as a morgue, 'the dead and dying huddled together indiscriminately in small filthy rooms.' The Governor, Sir Richard Macdonnell, one of the very first rulers of Hong Kong to recognize the Government's responsibility for the Chinese, gave his support to a movement now started amongst the rich Chinese merchants to found a hospital to replace the I Ts'z temple, the horrors of which had been given wide publicity in the Colony. The Chinese themselves contributed liberally, the Government gave a sum of money, and the Secretary of State for the Colonies authorized a large grant from the proceeds of gambling licences (which were then being officially farmed out but which were soon altogether suspended). The new hospital, the committee of which became, and has since remained, a very powerful influence in the life of the Chinese community of Hong Kong, was called Tung Wah and was opened by the Governor in 1872.

IV

In spite of the fact that only Chinese medicines were administered, and that operations were performed without chloroform but with the assistance of a dark-brown, aromatic powder which threw the patient into a deep sleep, the Tung Wah was from the first recognized by the British as a remarkable example of what the Chinese community of Hong Kong could, with official encouragement, achieve. It consisted of a series of two-storeyed granite buildings, well ventilated with large windows, a cross-current of air, and wards holding twenty patients each. These were divided into two-bedded stalls. The beds were wooden platforms, with wadded quilts washed weekly and pillows of bamboo. On a shelf above each bed was a teapot in a wadded basket, and a ticket showing the patient's name and the hours for his or her medication. The patients all lay with their backs to the light, with a space of five feet wide between beds and windows. Dry earth and sandalwood were used as deodorants and all the wards gave European visitors a distinct impression of efficiency and cleanliness. In the surgery no amputations were performed, but malignant growths were cut out and the wounds, dressed with musk, lard and ambergris, were sealed over with oiled paper. Musk and tiger's fat were employed in cases of gangrene, but the total absence of disinfectants made the surgery the only obnoxious part of the Tung Wah Hospital. In the 'chemical kitchen' eight cooks 'in spotless white clothing' superintended the concoction of medicines in one hundred and fifty earthen pipkins on a similar number of earthen stoves. The mortality at the Tung Wah was high, chiefly because it harboured the destitute and the moribund. A death-house into which no one but 'an unclean class of pariahs' would enter was rated by a British visitor in 1877 'a gloomy receptacle' but 'also clean'.

The same tourist, who was accompanying the Governor and the Anglican Bishop on a State visit to the Tung Wah, was equally impressed by the high-walled garden surrounding the hospital buildings, by the entrance paved with great granite flags, and by the grand staircase of the 'lofty central building'. This main building was a handsome hall, its roof supported on massive pillars, and with one side open to the garden. A great ebony table was used for board meetings, with a throne-like chair for the chairman and six carved ebony chairs on either side. On this State occasion the twelve directors and their chairman 'all wore rich and beautiful dresses of thick ribbed and figured brocade, and, unless they were much padded and wadded, they had all attained to a remarkable degree of embonpoint.'

The Tung Wah Hospital Committee soon branched out into other charitable activities; in 1898, for instance, it was running six free schools for poor children, 'in which the traditional Chinese education could be given without government grant or inspection'. It also became a political power, exerting its influence to settle strikes and to support the Government when it judged appropriate. The creation of the Tung Wah was an excellent instance of co-operation with the Government, which till then had done little of a paternalistic nature for the Hong Kong Chinese.

In post-war Hong Kong, the Tung Wah Group are now responsible for three hospitals: the Tung Wah itself, the Kwong Wah in Kowloon and the Tung Wah Eastern on Causeway Bay. All these are given Government subventions, and play their part with other hospitals and public and private clinics in helping to solve what would seem to be, with housing, the Colony's outstanding problem—the naturally high incidence, in such a vast and crowded population, of tuberculosis and venereal disease.

V

In one sense, the self-sufficiency and organizing gifts of the leaders of the Chinese community were a help to the Government—at any rate in the days when the population of the Colony was comparatively small. 'It is a much easier task to govern the twenty thousand Chinese inhabitants in this Colony, than the few hundreds of English,' Sir John Davis, the Colony's second Governor, wrote to the Secretary of State in 1844. But Sir John Davis, we may remember, was a sinologist who understood and liked the Chinese. And here we come to another reason for the Hong Kong Europeans' distrust of the Chinese—the language barrier. We have seen that, amongst Europeans generally, it was believed that a knowledge of the Chinese language warped the mind and unbalanced the judgment. We have also seen that to insist on the Chinese using that childish lingo, pidgin English, was considered preferable to any serious efforts to teach them good English. Now, a casual visitor to a country the language of which he does not understand can accept that fact with the amused resignation of a transient. But to form part of a business minority, which was also a ruling caste, in the midst of a vast population whose thoughts, feelings and reactions you cannot, through sheer ignorance, comprehend can only lead to a suspicious, jumpy state of mind. Official interpreters, however slick, may not invariably be reliable, and it is therefore extremely hard to fathom what is really going on. Even in modern Hong

Kong, where upper- and middle-class Chinese speak perfect English, the majority of the population speak no English at all. The most extroverted, the most smug or the most un-self-conscious Britisher cannot help wondering, while waiters giggle together in corners, or bank-clerks chirrup over cheques, whether they are not amusing themselves at his expense. If this is true today, how much more so must it have been true in the Hong Kong of the last century?

This potentially hopeless language situation would sometimes be exploited by astute British officials, who would answer Chinese grievances (through an interpreter) by pointing out that they had totally misunderstood the particular law or regulation of which they complained. A specialist in this art was Sir Richard MacDonnell, Governor of Hong Kong from 1866 to 1872. Although Sir Richard supported the Tung Wah Hospital project, and 'watched with an eagle's eye the editing of the Chinese issue of the Government Gazette', he was an adept at refuting the arguments of Chinese deputations to Government House and at forcing them to agree that he was right and they were wrong, and that the reason they were wrong was that his measures had been badly translated. Sir Richard 'invariably sent them away crestfallen'. But it was more usually the British officials who, in their state of linguistic siege, ended up in a baffled defeat.

This war of nerves between what was once called 'a firm European regime' and its subjects, the Chinese, was complicated, for successive Governors, by the resolute hostility of the British merchants to any mild official measures to promote real Chinese interests and to redress legitimate grievances. The war still goes on. An eye-witness of the riots of the summer of 1967, which were partially Maoist in origin, I found few people who would admit that they were really caused by vile living and working conditions, by lack of good labour-management relations, and by the Government's tenacity in clinging, in a modern world, to the outworn principles on which Hong Kong was founded—those of non-interference or *laissez-faire*. These principles created hardship enough in the days when Hong Kong was the commercial emporium of the East. Now, when it is also an expanding industrial centre, they seem perilously and, indeed, criminally out of date.

VI

To anyone at all acquainted with Hong Kong's past—with the various histories of the Colony which have from time to time been written, with the official dispatches in the Public Record Office in Chancery Lane, or with the files of local newspapers in the British Museum's stacks at Colindale—the summer of 1967 was a season of peculiar significance. Strikes, riots and other forms of racial unrest have periodically disrupted the life of Hong Kong; but, like the destructive typhoons and the epidemics which the Colony has often endured, these misfortunes have been taken, by successive Governments, in their stride. The demonstrations of 1967, on the other hand, were immediately recognized as something new—and something ominous as well. Rumour, which has always played an inordinate part in Hong Kong life, ran amok. European husbands began urging their wives to pack up, take the children, and flee. Rich Chinese and Eurasians would make sudden, unexplained visits to San Francisco or to Switzerland. Profound disquiet reigned. The riot police, helmeted and efficient, with their circular black wicker shields making them look like Roman legionaries, became the heroes of the hour. A public subscription was opened for the higher education of their children, and the English-language newspapers vied with one another in compliments to the police of Hong Kong. Taken altogether, the summer riots of 1967 were a phenomenon which no one could ignore. Instead of being confined, like previous demonstrations, to Kowloon-side or to the slummier parts of Victoria, some of these riots defiantly took place in the very centre of the capital, outside the great banks and American hotels, outside Government House itself.

Government House, Victoria, was reconstructed by the Japanese during their military occupation of the Colony in the Second World War. Save for an inexplicable and redundant tower, they carried out this rebuilding in a sensibly unpretentious manner. 'G.H.' had always been a modest, but roomy and convenient sort of house, described by one of its nineteenth-century inmates as 'a model residence for a tropical climate' and 'far superior, indeed, as regards comfort' to many more grandiose and costly Governors' residences which were at one time springing up throughout the British Empire—such, for instance, as that facing the Port of Spain savannah in Trinidad. There was a flat roof from which a fine view across the town and over the harbour was available, and which members of the Governor's family would use when convalescent or seeking protective solitude. The two acres of grounds contain tennis courts, a shady garden and many flowering shrubs.

Across the way from the front gates of Government House, and higher up the hillside, is one of the prettiest sights of Victoria—the Botanical Gardens. This charming example of an art-form at which the old British colonial Governments particularly excelled was planned in 1861. It was an imaginative venture, since it had to be hacked out of the solid rock, bedded with deep soil, and then stocked with rare seeds and plants sent out from Kew Gardens and from Australia. This arboreal activity was soon imitated by private people in the vicinity, as well as by municipal plantings such as the firs and eucalyptus trees on Mount Davis and on the slopes above Kennedy Road. When, in 1864, the new Botanical Gardens were opened to the public, promenade concerts given in them by military bands became a regular, enlivening feature of Hong Kong life. Unlike the City Museum and Library the Botanical Gardens opposite Government House were from the very start public and open to all races.

I stood, one May morning of 1967, under a shady tree in these Botanical Gardens, looking down at the tumult below. It was an interesting and unusual spectacle, and was, in a sense, the siege of Government House. Walking up Garden Road from Central in the comparative cool of the early morning (before the sun had really got down to work) I had been passed by long, orderly crocodiles of students and schoolchildren clad in white, each of them armed with a scarlet-bound copy of the thoughts of Mao; and all converging on Government House. As I drifted leisurely up the steep, winding road I could hear shouting, a blurred noise that became sharper and louder as I ascended the hill, until it turned into a species of Bastille roar. Rounding the corner I came on several thousand Chinese demonstrators brandishing their little books and chanting Mao's thoughts. There were police in posses. Television and newspaper reporters would suddenly be attacked by members of the crowd without warning; it was on the whole a rhythmic scene only interrupted by scuffles over attempts to smash press cameras or to push back the riot police. The tall iron gates of Government House were locked with a chain and the house itself, with closed jalousies, seemed lifeless. The sentry was in his sentry-box. The Union Jack on the G.H. roof stirred from time to time in a puff of breeze from the sea. All over the gates, the neighbouring trees and the sentry-box were pink-and-white Maoist posters. These leaflets, which from the vertiginous positions of some of them at least gave proof of the gymnastic energy of Chinese youth, were removed by the police each evening and replaced by the rioters next day. The demonstrators were asking to see the Governor who, rightly or wrongly, did not appear. It was a scene which Government House, Hong Kong, had never witnessed before.

What we were ourselves witnessing on this, and other, mornings seemed to me to be the murder of a myth—the myth of a loyal and contented Chinese community living happily under the rule of a benevolent British Government. Even Government officials could no longer go on pretending that working conditions in Hong Kong are not, for the majority of the population, virtually intolerable. When Lord Shepherd, Minister of State at the Commonwealth Office in Mr Harold Wilson's Government, paid a lightning visit to investigate what was really happening in the Colony, he issued an interesting statement. This was to the effect that he had initiated discussions with management in Hong Kong on 'the questions of giving men employees the right to one day's holiday a week'. Hours of work for women and young persons were to be reduced from sixty hours a week to forty-eight. This indictment of factory conditions could also have been extended to other money-making concerns—in particular to Hong Kong restaurants in which, to my own knowledge, most young waiters work incredibly long hours and have exactly four days holiday a year. There were three stock official answers to any inquiries I happened to make about, say, restaurant working hours. The Chinese, I was told, like overworking; it would be impossible to devise legislation to control restaurant hours; and, even if such legislation were at all feasible, it would be, with Hong Kong's great pool of unemployment, impossible to enforce, since restaurant-keepers could easily find fresh employees who would work the old excessive hours without lodging any complaints. In Hong Kong, in fact, the tenets of the mill-owners of Victorian England still prevail.

The real anxiety, indeed the real fear, which the 1967 riots aroused, however, was political rather than social in origin. It was, quite simply, the fear of Maoist China, and the uncertainty of whether the Hong Kong demonstrations were the work of local agitators merely, or were being skilfully directed from Peking. Behind this fear and this uncertainty lay the grudging recognition that the emporium of the East today exists on the sufferance of Red China and could at any moment be conquered and absorbed, The largest area of the Colony will, in any case, revert to the Government of China when the ninety-nine-year lease of the New Territories lapses in less than thirty years' time. What are the 'New Territories' and when and why were they acquired?

VII

With the addition of the New Territories, comprising an area of the Chinese mainland three hundred and sixty-five square miles in size and also a number of offshore islands, the whole ethos of the Crown Colony of Hong Kong was changed. Up to 1898, the year in which the lease of the New Territories was signed with the Chinese Government, Hong Kong had been, as we have seen, an increasingly prosperous free port, an island mart. The acquisition, in 1860, of Kowloon and of Stonecutter's Island had been primarily dictated by military considerations, the object being to make Hong Kong Island secure from Chinese attack. But by the 'nineties of the last century China, in a state of near chaos, no longer seemed a potential threat; what was now feared was an attack by a European power—France, Russia or Germany, all of which were now expanding their interests in the Far East. France, in particular, was acquiring territorial and other concessions in South China, and it was to forestall a French presence on the coastline opposite Hong Kong island that Joseph Chamberlain, then Secretary of State for the Colonies, agreed to negotiate the lease of the New Territories for a period of ninety-nine years.

The very name, New Territories, which Hong Kong people today take for granted, is misleading; for what the

British obtained in 1898 was a region populated since time immemorial by Chinese landlords and peasants, and containing old walled villages and ancient temples. It was an area which had always been a trouble to the Emperor's viceroys at Canton, a scene of fierce village feuds and divided loyalties. The then Governor of Hong Kong, another southern Irishman, Sir Henry Blake, soon found that, though villages in the New Territories might squabble and fight between one another, there was a more or less united feeling of resentment at the arrival of the British. Police and troops sent from the Colony were sporadically resisted by units of the Chinese army, and it was not until the end of April 1899 that the British military occupation of the New Territories was complete. Although the New Territories were deemed strategically necessary to Hong Kong, and although coal was discovered at Deep Bay and a concession for it granted to Jardine Matheson, the Hong Kong Government had in fact taken on a set of completely new administrative problems and responsibilities for which its original constitution had never been designed. The post of Governor of Hong Kong was thus made a far more ticklish one than ever before, since it now involved the control of alien-occupied territory, every bit as much as the extension of British rule from the Gold Coast forts up to the kingdom of Ashanti in 1901. Hong Kong thus became yet another example of a new theme of British Empire, by which possessions which had begun as small, a-political trading stations were now seen to involve inevitable territorial expansion on a large scale. There was now a long border with China to be controlled, complex systems of customs dues to be negotiated, land revenue to be collected and new roads to be built. A railway was constructed from Kowloon running over the border as far as Canton. This railway, on which modern Hong Kong depends for the bulk of its foodstuffs, incidentally puts the Colony's welfare at the mercy of the Chinese Government, for, as they did for some days in the summer troubles of 1967, that Government can refuse to run any food trains into Hong Kong. A good enough military project in its day, the lease of the New Territories was, therefore, politically a dubious blessing. Today, with the great Plover Cove reservoir scheme being pushed rapidly forward, and beautiful roads and model factories, this area of the Colony gives an impression of permanence and progress, although the lease of it will expire in the year 1997.

6

VISUALS

I

WE have now, I think, reached a point in this biographical essay on Hong Kong at which the reasons for the Crown Colony's original existence and gradual expansion should be clear. I trust that the reader will likewise have grasped at least some of the problems and difficulties—population explosion, race relations, language barriers, archaic constitution, selfish business interests—with which successive British Governors have had to grapple for more than one hundred and twenty-five years. I have so far stressed the social and historical aspects of Hong Kong at the expense of the Colony's visual aspects, save when I have emphasized my own personal distaste for the ant-hill quality of life in the streets and tenements and shack-dwellings of Victoria and Kowloon, and, on the other hand, my personal liking for the island's bays and capes and sunsets. To offset the somewhat gloomy picture which I have drawn it would seem both fair and necessary to consider here the features of real beauty and interest still to be found in Hong Kong. We may begin with a brief look at the New Territories.

Despite their speedy development and the giant dams

and excavations which are, of necessity, ruining the pastoral beauty of Plover Cove, walks in the New Territories reveal to you living relics of a fourteenth-century world, and give you an authentic sense of being inside the old China of the Emperors. There are ancient villages and monasteries and temples. You can wander along the raised mud dykes of the Sha Tin valley between paddy fields and marrow fields, and fields of brilliant white and purple asters in flower. Women and girls in black tunics and black trousers, wearing great cartwheel hats of black straw edged with pelmets of black smocked cotton against the sun, work stooping in the fields and cry out to one another raucously. In this particular valley, justly famous for its beauty, are sixteen Buddhist monasteries. Away on a bleak hillside stands a solitary boulder, shaped like a woman carrying a child, and called in English 'The Amah Rock'—but its Chinese name means 'Hoping Husband Returns' and is connected with a thirteenth-century legend of a lady who spent years waiting for the return of her warrior husband; but, when he did finally come back from Canton, she died of joy. In the valley below are some more holy boulders, huddled beneath an aged, contorted tree, in the twisted roots of which you can find joss-sticks burning, as mysterious as the lonely fetishes beside the roads of the West Indies or West Africa, or the wands by the Irish wishing-wells. Farther on is a Buddhist temple attached to a monastery and old people's home. It stands behind a lofty green-painted iron gate and in a garden of camellia trees. You are admitted to the garden by a Chinese crone in a turban, an old lady with only three teeth, but each of them is gold. There are young monks with saffron robes and shaven heads. Inside, the little temple is cold and peaceful, garish with red lacquer and embroidered scarlet banners, lamps dimly twinkling and the usual scent of stale incense in the air.

The Sha Tin valley encloses an arm of Mirs Bay, and many well-to-do Chinese and Eurasian families have now built modern houses with fine gardens on the hillsides, commanding splendid views down over this placid sheet of water and of the hills upon the farther side. Both in the New Territories and on Hong Kong Island itself, such private dwellings are constructed with an eye not only to the view but also to the correct orientation of the house according to Fung Shui. No Chinese or Eurasian would dream of building a new house without first consulting a soothsayer, a man trained to choose a propitious site and to decide which way the house should face. Fung Shui, in which these soothsayers are experts, is a complicated influence which can bring you happiness and prosperity if good, and ruin you if bad. A house near a river, for example, must, according to Fung Shui, face upstream, as otherwise the water will carry your livelihood away. Graves also are positioned by similar considerations, and have to be set at a certain angle of the hillsides on which they are traditionally built. But even Fung Shui experts have been known to make mistakes (rather as water-diviners sometimes do so in the West) and these result in a costly reconstruction of the new edifice when the error has been belatedly discovered and the house recognized as standing, say, on a dragon's head.

The cult of the dragon in Chinese mythology is, apparently, obscure in origin but potent in fact. At the midsummer solstice is celebrated the Dragon Boat Festival, the second of the three annual festivals of the living and at the same time the festival of fishermen. In the waters of the Sha Tin valley the most important of the Dragon Boat Races to mark this festival is held. Hot, noisy and hysterical, it did not seem to me to bear any comparison with another festival, held in spring, in another charming part of the New Territories, the island of Cheung Chau. With their gift for domesticating the exotic, and for rendering the mysterious prosaic, English residents and the English-language newspapers refer to this gay and gaudy celebration, all shining gilt and acrid scarlets and almond greens and virulent magentas, as the 'Bun Feast'. But called by any name it is well worth going to watch.

II

Cheung Chau is a small island lying eight miles south-west of Hong Kong proper, and like Lantau and Lamma and a clutch of other islets it formed part of the package-deal of the New Territories in 1898. The number of Europeans actually living on Cheung Chau is, I believe, negligible. The island thus remains wholly Chinese in character and atmosphere, and the day spent at the festival there gave me more of a sense of being in the Orient than I had had since, the week previously, I had left Japan. The narrow shopping lanes through which the procession jerkily meandered bore very little sign of a British presence, save perhaps for the policemen who were trying to keep it orderly and for some of the more lurid plastic objects in the crammed, open-fronted shops.

I had been invited to Cheung Chau by some acquaintances who lease a motorized junk. The Hong Kong junk has long become, for tourists, a picturesque symbol to be found on a myriad coloured postcards and in the illustrations to the limited number of books which, over the years, the Colony has inspired. Seen from my hotel window at Repulse Bay, or from some point along the coastal road upon the cliffs, these junks do indeed, to the inexperienced eye, look graceful and romantic, as they seem to scud upon the surface of the green-blue sea. At night, when their owners set off for distant fishing-grounds with flares or twinkling lanterns in the bows, you have a firefly scene which has been only too persistently described as 'bejewelled'. Yet the junks of Hong Kong are as much a source of livelihood as the pedlar's motor van or the totter's cart. They are likewise mobile houses in which, in an inconceivably restricted and well-planned space, whole generations of fisher-people live, cook, eat, give birth and rear their progeny. Junks need the greatest skill in handling, and the brown sails, which, seen from the shore, have the veined fragility of dead autumn leaves, are in reality tough yet flexible and strain in the wind as though they were going to burst. Junks do not really skim or scud, they heave or rock as they breast the waves. Being on board a junk instead of seeing one at a convenient distance might in fact be compared to going backstage at a theatre after you have been bewitched by the illusion of a play. A fishing junk is one of the most practical, demanding and least picturesque of boats—but none the less agreeable for that.

The harbour of Cheung Chau is a forest of junk-masts; really a marine extension of the land. We moored out in the harbour and took a sampan to the jetty. Scrambling up this you were immediately aware of two main factors of the festival—firstly the lilting, cacophonous sound of eastern flutes, cymbals and drums, and, secondly, the impressive but somehow childish spectacle of three towering conical pyramids, standing side by side beneath a temporary roof. These pyramids, of scaffolding sixty feet high, were covered with a sheath of ovoid, pinkish objects, like small smooth boulders or large goose-eggs. They were arranged with that minute, almost architectural, care which the Chinese bring to the display of every species of merchandise, and they tapered upwards in perfect symmetry. These cakes—or, as the Europeans will have it, these 'buns' —are heavy and indigestible. Since this is one of the three Chinese festivals dedicated to death, the cakes form an offering to the spirits of the dead. At dusk on the fourth and final day of the festival a priest decides when the spirits have eaten enough, and the young fishermen clamber swiftly up the pyramids to seize the cakes which are then distributed amongst the onlookers. According to Dr Ommanney the 'Bun Feast' is also 'a fast in expiation of the lives of creatures taken during the past year in order to provide mankind with his daily bread'. No animals are slaughtered during the four-day celebrations, no fishing-boats put out to sea, and the island restaurants serve only vegetarian food 'except for oysters which may be eaten because, as everybody knows, they have no souls'.

Beyond the cake pyramids, that glaring afternoon, the piazza of the town was hemmed in by spectators, tiptoeing to watch the long procession which was winding its way from the Temple of Jade Vacuity into the narrow main street of the town. This temple, which faces the sea, has stone steps leading up to it and is guarded by porcelain lions. Inside, it is murky and ill-kept, smelling of joss-sticks and with its untidy main altar dedicated to Pei Ti, the Supreme God of Profound Heaven. For the festival, this god, with a number of others, is carried through the town in a form of litter, preceded and followed by lion dancers, shadow-boxers, youths playing musical instruments and small, painted and richly dressed children carried aloft on poles. These children, who are seated on little chairs which their long satin robes conceal, have a wonderful air of immobility and at first sight seem to be life-size dolls. After the procession is over, the gods and goddesses are placed in matshed tents backing on the sea and facing the temple. To their right a large temporary theatre offers a wailing Chinese opera.

This, the first large Chinese festival in which I had participated, had all the flashing elements of colour, gaiety and sheer noise which shelvesful of European travel-books on China have described. But to me it was, primarily, bewildering. The more its varied meanings were explained to one, the more inexplicable it began to seem to be. Like many other inquisitive Europeans I have, at one time and another, tried reading books on Buddhism—desultorily, perhaps, but with a true wish to understand its tenets and its ramifications. My good intentions have always been thwarted and my efforts have never been a success. The temples of the Sha Tin valley, the Temple of Jade Vacuity in Cheung Chau, the temples that I saw on Hong Kong Island and the temples that I saw at Macao only served to increase my sense of defeat. Certain absolute deities, like the Goddess of Mercy, become recognizable upon their altars; but others change their mission and even their sex according to locality, and become as complex and elusive as the Chinese cosmology itself.

III

In contrast to the mainland and the islets of the New Territories, where patient investigation on foot or by motor-car is rewarded by many sights of romantic detail, the finest visual impressions of Hong Kong Island itself are those which are in a sense generalized and seen from a distance—in the early morning, at dusk, or at night. The best view of the harbour and the indented, curving coast-line, for instance, is that obtained from the summit of the eighteen-hundred-foot mountain which dominates Victoria city, and which is colloquially known to all residents as 'The Peak'.

The Peak, or more correctly Victoria Peak, is the highest and most prominent mountain on this mountainous island. You can reach its summit nowadays by a good motor-road, but it is far more amusing to take a ticket on the Peak Tramway, opened in 1897, which hauls you up the steep hillside from the centre of Victoria, and deposits you at a car park near the summit. Here there is one of those viewing telescopes popular in Switzerland, and you can survey the whole fine harbour massed with shipping. Up here too is a Chinese restaurant where you can sit in the shady garden, among the frangipani, the hibiscus and the bright, lazy butterflies. Except at week-ends, this Peak restaurant forms a quiet refuge from the city below. The steep, spasmodic journey of the tramcars, stopping at little precipitous wayside stations, and giving you glimpses of the backs of houses, washing on lines and people's gardens, has an intimate charm of its own. The passengers, whether daily commuters, amahs with children, or tourists, can be studied at close range and as isolated individuals, which is not really possible in the tumult of Victoria's streets, or even on the giant ferries to Kowloon. This Peak tramway and its toy halts belong to an older, earlier version of Hong Kong.

The Peak is now, to say the least of it, fully inhabited, with the usual blocks of Hong Kong flats and some private houses. Its drawback is that common to all subtropical mountain tops—for months at a time it is cloaked in a damp white mist, which swirls and eddies round it so that you cannot see the view, destroys books and shoes, and drives the residents to keep their clothes and linen in 'hot-cupboards'. But even with the mist at its worst the air is at least cool; and in summer-time you can actually go so far as to think up there, without feeling that your brain is bursting or addled with the humid heat.

It was Sir Hercules Robinson, the Governor who lost his dispute with the Army about Kowloon, who first urged Hong Kong Europeans to spend summers on the Peak. At this time 'the sanitary aspects' even of the Peak were dubiously regarded by the foreign community, and a military sanatorium on the summit had been abandoned. Robinson arranged to take over this site from the Army authorities, had a path hacked from Victoria upwards through the scrub, and planned a summer bungalow for the use of the Governor or his officials which became known as Mountain Lodge. This building, destroyed in the 1874 hurricane and rebuilt with a cement hurricane cellar, was once more obliterated during the Japanese invasion of 1941. All that remains of the bungalow, up to which Governors of my grandfather's era would be carried in their litter by scarlet-clad bearers, is a large tessellated floor, the typhoon cellar and some urns. A walk leads from it through what appears to be the remains of a garden. At the end of the walk is a circular stone table engraved with geographical information such as the exact distance to Peking. From the point on which this table is placed you gain a superb view of the sea and the islands—when, that is to say, the summit is not swathed in the wayward rags and tatters of cold white mist.

A detailed and somewhat gruesome account of life at Mountain Lodge, to be found in the autobiography of a Governor who ran the Colony from 1887 till 1891, lends support to my private axiom that some people can never win out in Hong Kong. Sir William des Voeux described life on the Peak as 'trying to the patience' during the period 'when clouds rested upon it'.

> In our first year [he records] this happened but rarely, and never lasted more than a day or two. But in our second season it was very different, and this miserable experience lasted for the greater part of the summer. On one occasion, for several weeks together, the fog was as dense as the worst which afflicts London in November, and only differed from it as being white instead of brown. The damp inside the house was such that water ran down the walls in streams and collected in pools on the polished floors. Such indeed was the moisture in the air that bed linen had to be kept in a

> hot drying-room, and would become too wet to sleep in if taken out more than a few minutes before it was required to be used. At such times one seemed entirely cut off from the rest of the world, the existence of which was revealed only at rare intervals by the arrival of a Government messenger with papers, or by the clicking of the telephone.

Sir William explains that when this was the state of the atmosphere on the Peak 'the heat in the town below was usually at its greatest', but that, all the same, he found going to his office 'a welcome change'.

> Occasionally [he continues] after many days in succession of a life which resembled that of a damp and gloomy prison, we would go for a change down to sleep for a night or two at our house in town. It was a pleasure to see daylight and bright sky again, but the heat, which rendered sleep almost impossible, quickly drove us up again.

Up on the Peak the des Voeux gave, weather permitting, weekly garden parties, when the guests—mainly Peak residents—would disport themselves on two good lawn-tennis courts attached to Mountain Lodge. He describes the narrow twin verandas, which bounded the house on north and south. That on the north side looked out directly on to the very tiptop of the Peak, a quarter of a mile away, on which was a signal station used to signal the approach of vessels, and the names of the firms for which they were carrying their consignments. The southern veranda, however, commanded 'a magnificent prospect over the China Sea, comprehending a long line of mountainous coast and innumerable islands'. On fine evenings the gubernatorial family would sit and watch the sunsets (which indeed are, in Hong Kong, of extraordinary variety and beauty) and, after nightfall, the constellations of the stars—'from that spot neither sight nor sound gave any token of human existence, and it seemed difficult to realize that within so short a distance was a dense population.'

Today, as I have said, the Peak is itself a fairly densely residential area; but walking in the wilderness of the old garden of Mountain Lodge, and gazing down at the harbour lights by night, or at the capes and bays of the island at early morning, is far and away one of the most impressive and moving experiences that modern Hong Kong can still provide.

IV

One of the greatest scenic pleasures Hong Kong Island affords the stranger is, as I have suggested in the preliminary section of this book, driving along the sinuous coastal roads, which mount and dip with the contours of the hills, and provide a splendid seascape of green-blue waters marbled by cloud reflections and almost littered with little dark islets between which junks and yachts are always on the move. Some of these islets are British-controlled, others, perilously close to the Colony, belong to the Communist Chinese. This fine road system is being constantly improved, but in fact represents a gradual development, over the decades, of a surprisingly ambitious and imaginative circular road plan initiated immediately the British had acquired Hong Kong. Rough roads and bridle paths, which, like the wooden bridges, often could not withstand the summer rains, were laid out. They connected the capital with the handful of seaside fishing hamlets which already existed on the island, and which were soon re-christened with English names. Chek Chue, on the south-east coast, became Stanley, after Lord Stanley, the Secretary of State for War and the Colonies when the Treaty of Nanking was ratified, whilst the junk village of Chek Py Wan farther to the west was now called Aberdeen, after the Secretary of State for Foreign Affairs in the same Cabinet. Detachments of troops under canvas were stationed at both these places, and police stations were erected to try to control the questionable activities of the junk people, who were known to combine fishing with piracy. This anglicization of Chinese place-names was thorough, but many of them, even amongst the English, did not catch on. No one nowadays would seriously call Kong Sin Wan 'Telegraph Bay' or the charming Chinese village of Shek O, so popular in summer-time, by its English version, 'Rocky Bay'. In Victoria itself the districts have some a Chinese name, others an English one. Thus Wanchai is next to Central, Quarry Bay next to Shau Kei Wan, there are Happy Valley and Pokfulam, for as the new city grew it engulfed purely Chinese settlement areas. Although the *apartheid* pattern of Hong Kong living has long since ceased, and Chinese can live wherever they like if they can afford to do so, there are certain places, both in the city and in rural areas, which remain, in character, irrevocably Chinese. One of these is the fishing port, or village, of Aberdeen.

Aberdeen is a settlement of junk-dwellers, fishing families who live aboard their moored boats and who for generations have never conceived what it could be like to live on land. The village lies, or, rather, bobs and floats on a fine harbour on the south coast of the island westward of Stanley and of Repulse Bay. In a sense Aberdeen is another of these Hong Kong places which are seen at their best from a distance, in this case from a certain point on the road to Repulse Bay. In the midst of the junks which, with their tapering masts, resemble a crowded plantation of raffish young pine trees, two large, ornate and vividly painted Chinese restaurants are tethered. Offering excellent Cantonese sea-food and a view down on to the junk families, with their cooking utensils, bedding, children and chow-dogs all fitted in like pieces of a jig-saw puzzle, these restaurant-barges are a tourist Mecca. At night, from the Repulse Bay road, they shine under the moon like giant Chinese lanterns, glowing with coloured lights. But sanitation seems to be the major problem of the junk people, and the picturesque, Chinnery-like scene is marred by the assault of strange and unattractive smells, as well as by the human excreta making a scum on the surface of the green water. The sunlit waterfront of Aberdeen echoes and re-echoes with perpetual and mystifying Chinese laughter—mystifying chiefly because there would not, at first sight, seem to me much about life in this water-borne slum to evoke merriment. Sampans wait along the quay like taxis waiting for hire and the sampan girls compete fiercely for the custom of anyone showing any sign of wishing to cross over to the floating restaurants; they almost drag you into the sampan, which wobbles jerkily over the water to deliver its passengers at the foot of the rocking steps of one or other of the two restaurants.

An efficient land reclamation scheme, to support yet

more cement tenement towers and to rehouse the junk-people, is now in progress, although the junk-owners and their families are supposed to be reluctant to abandon the floating homes of their tradition to settle prosaically on dry land. I was told that in order to feel at home some of the newly rehoused had set about building junk decks in their new apartments, but whether this was one of the myths of the innate quaintness of the Chinese character or an absolute fact I could never ascertain. On land Aberdeen has a large market-place, as animated and bustling as all markets in the East, and some good shops. In spite of the dirt, and the stench of drying fish, Aberdeen is worth frequenting and is, in its own way, a sympathetic, animated little place.

The road eastward from Aberdeen carries you past Repulse Bay and on to the township of Stanley, formerly Chek Chue, which straddles a thin peninsula. Repulse Bay, where I was staying in an excellent hotel, with wide verandas, an avenue of flame-trees in flower, and an outlook on to the bay and the hump of Middle Island in the foreground, is perhaps the most superb in an island of superb bays, though here, too, the white towers are rising on every hand, and the hillsides above it are raw orange from the excavation of yet more building-sites. Stanley itself really comprises two separate towns—the original fishing hamlet of Chek Chue, low down by the waters of the Chek Chue Wan, and a more sophisticated, indeed luxurious, section of rich villas with lovely, somehow secret flower-gardens, overlooking the other side of the peninsula, on Tai Tam Bay. Beyond Stanley the road climbs sharply along the grey-green, scrub-covered heights above the bay. This seems to me to be by far the most spectacular drive on the island.

The old part of Stanley, that on the Chek Chue Wan, has a charming, sleazy little market-place by the shore. Here a shapeless complex of stalls kept by trousered women sell the usual assortment of goods—enamel basins, shirts, bathing trunks, cotton dresses and children's toys. The immense quantities of cheap toys for sale in Hong Kong are the product of one of the Colony's major industries but also, I fancy, reflect that particular tendency amongst Chinese of all classes to lavish affection on their children in a way reminiscent of Italian parents. The early life of the Chinese child is, in fact, one of enviable ease. Strapped to the back of its mother, its older sister or its grandmother, it surveys the world from a grown-up's eye-level, and can drop off to sleep whenever it wishes. It has food popped into its mouth with chopsticks and, when old enough to scramble about, is encouraged to play as much as possible. For a bright child the parent, however impoverished, will concentrate on saving money for a good education—since it is realized that only by this means can the child rise into the respected, money-making group of office or Government workers or shop assistants. A Chinese childhood in Hong Kong would seem to be, on the whole, a carefree and protected affair.

Stanley market, which is a microcosm of the huge market-places of Victoria and Kowloon, is, like them, equipped with instant food—cauldrons bubbling in the shade of corrugated iron sheds, heavy-looking cakes, li-chees, oranges and so on. There are pungent smells of spice and curry, and sheltered tables at which people sit and eat. In marked contrast to the unplanned, casual look of the market, which appears to have been dumped at the foot of its hill, is the other side of the Stanley Peninsula—the spacious villas, the flower-gardens, the shadowy verandas. These houses are built and inhabited by well-to-do Europeans, Eurasians and Chinese. Near Stanley is a military camp, used by the Japanese as an internment camp during the Second World War, and also what is probably the best school in the island, modelled on the system of the English public-school.

If you continue driving eastward from Stanley, along a road which goes first uphill, then along a ridge, and soon cuts inland, you drop down on another fine bay, that of Shek O. This region also has big private villas, and boasts a golf-course and a country club. But what is nicest about it, I think, is the purely Chinese hamlet of Shek O itself, consisting of three or four sandy streets, a few open-fronted shops, some small Chinese private houses protected by padlocked gates or barbed wire, a gaudy little Buddhist temple and a Roman Catholic chapel. There are several open-air restaurants which cater for the Sunday invasion of the city Chinese who, in summer-time, avail themselves in swarms of the recent permission to swim from beaches previously reserved for Europeans. There is one particularly charming small hotel, protected from the sea-winds by a catalpa grove full of tiny tables at which people sit loudly playing mahjong, clacking the green-backed mahjong pieces and shouting with merriment. By the side of the little hotel is a dim, sunless garden where flowering plants are rather desperately growing. The village curs lope by below the veranda, hens peck in the dust, and you feel that you could sit there for ever gazing vaguely out to sea.

V

If, at Shek O or on the very summit of the Peak, you can temporarily forget the buzzing streets of Victoria, this is even more true if you are lucky enough to penetrate into the spacious and hospitable old mansions of rich Hong Kong Eurasians or Chinese. In these private houses you find a calm and a privacy which, in Hong Kong, only money can buy and here you feel that the fortunes made in merchandise and banking have been put to a smooth and civilized use. There is something very characteristic of old Hong Kong about these houses. Furnished in the Western taste of seventy or eighty years ago, they could not, however, really be mistaken for the houses of Europeans. One room, for example, is set aside as the family shrine, with an altar and lacquer alcove dedicated to the domestic gods, gilt figurines which seem to exude benevolence and a sense of another world than this. These family shrines, the equivalent of family chapels in old houses in Spain or Italy, are not, of course, confined to the well-to-do. The poorest tenement room or flatlet would not only be incomplete but virtually uninhabitable without some shrine, however modest, for the Kitchen God, who is enthroned above the hearth, or over a lintel, or as one of the assemblage of deities in the family shrine. It is known that each New Year this god leaves the family he has been protecting, to report to heaven on their behaviour during the past year. But in the large private houses, the altars have representatives of several other deities to guard the family and home.

Some of the big Chinese houses, such as Eculiffe on

Repulse Bay, and Euston in Victoria itself, are rigid interpretations of European styles: others have the blue or green tiled roofs and turned-up eaves of traditional Chinese architecture. Such houses as Eucliffe are, to the European eye, misleading—for, although looking as though it had been designed for Sir Walter Scott, this granite monument to the taste of the Gothic Revival was in fact built in the nineteen thirties by the late millionaire, Mr Eu. With its turrets, massive walls, arrow-slits and heavy gates, Eucliffe gives an impression of solidity and safety. The cool living-rooms look out over the bay, and you have tea on the paved veranda. The garden has turfed courtyards at various levels. Inside the house are suits of armour, and paintings of nude European women. This taste for pictures and marble statues of Western nudes seems to have been widespread among Chinese millionaires of a generation or two back, and they can even be seen in Chinese villas in Kuala Lumpur in Malaya. As works of art they have no rating, and they make a voluptuous contrast to the domestic shrine-gods. They must have seemed a licentious status symbol when first shipped out to Hong Kong.

The modern houses of Hong Kong, such as those at Stanley, and one which has just been built by a Chinese friend of mine on Black's Gap Road above Deepwater Bay, are well designed, elegant and immensely comfortable. They are, as I have said earlier, built with an eye not only to Fung Shui, but also to the outward view over the South China Sea. One can sit in a garden or on some terrace balustraded with blue faience pilasters (still cast in Communist Canton) and relish, towards twilight, what I persist in regarding as the rarest and greatest of all the luxuries of

Police, with trained tracker dogs, patrol a Hong Kong street in search of drug-pedlars and their clients

The escape from reality: opium smokers in Hong Kong today

The frontier rail crossing-point between the New Territories and Red China. Until recent years refugees from Red China swarmed across this frontier

A street-market in Kowloon, showing tenement blocks erected to cope with the influx of refugees

Hong Kong police dealing with the outbreak of serious rioting in May 1967. The conduct of the police won high praise from the merchant community

Hong Kong—the sense of well-guarded privacy and the sense of air and space.

VI

Until 1967, there existed one easy solution for residents or visitors who found the commercial atmosphere of Hong Kong island beginning to oppress them, and who longed for respite. Their practice, on such occasions, was to cross the mouth of the Pearl River to spend a few days in the ancient Portuguese colony of Macao, only forty miles away. Some went there to gamble; some on other pleasures bent; and some simply to breathe a draught of air from Latin Europe, and to explore the rococo churches, the arcaded streets, the gardens of the Bishops' Palace on the top of Penha Hill, or the old English cemetery by the offices of the former East India Company. 'If you want to see what this Colony must have been like in the old days', an intelligent English transient told me during my first visit to Hong Kong in 1959, 'you had better leave the island at once and go over to Macao'. Baffled by the paradox that the best way to find out about one place was to leave it for another, I ignored this advice at that time. In the summer of 1967, however, I remembered it, and took the hydrofoil to Macao. By that time the Portuguese Government of the Colony had virtually capitulated to the demands of Communist Chinese, and shops, walls, convents, even the splendid façade of the ruined rococo church of Sao Paolo, destroyed by fire in 1837, were coated with pink Communist posters similar to those which the police were nightly removing from the streets and public buildings of Hong

Kong. The big hydrofoil was almost empty, and at the ferry station on the Praya Grande lines of empty taxis and pedicabs hopefully waited, while the city itself seemed to be quietly dying. Carmelite nuns were being evacuated on instructions from Lisbon, and the Bishop had temporarily left the Colony. But even in this pathetic and moribund state Macao remained beguiling and one could readily understand its perennial appeal to the inhabitants of the affluent society of Hong Kong. Here the oriental-picturesque had lingered, here was a sense of the past for which I had sought vainly on the island of Hong Kong.

You may object that an ancient Portuguese colony, founded in 1557 and still retaining a lazy and seductive Latin air, can never have had much in common with a British trading venture like Hong Kong, a city fashioned by hard-headed merchants and by bland missionaries of the Anglican persuasion. Superficially you would be right, for this small rococo town, with its myriad churches and gambling-dens and brothels, is indeed, as W. H. Auden has described it, 'a weed from Catholic Europe':

> A weed from Catholic Europe, it took root
> Between some yellow mountains and a sea,
> Its gay stone houses an exotic fruit,
> A Portugal-cum-China oddity.
>
> Rococo images of Saint and Saviour
> Promise its gamblers fortunes when they die,
> Churches alongside brothels testify
> That faith can pardon natural behaviour.

Yet, before the birth of Hong Kong, Macao, a haphazard amalgam of Chinese, Japanese and Portuguese cultures, was the Mecca of the British merchants in Canton. Like their French and American colleagues and rivals, they would retire to Macao for what is in current American army jargon called 'Rest and Recreation'. Almost all of these British merchants from Canton kept permanent houses in Macao. These were bachelor establishments smoothly run by a pretty Portuguese, Chinese or Japanese mistress, in the days before the mem sahib had descended on South-East Asia, bringing with her the prim and arid standards of the nineteenth-century Victorian housewife. These celibate establishments were conducted upon ample lines, with upwards of twenty servants, spanking horses to ride and, in some cases, a carriage and pair. This was the scene which George Chinnery recorded during his residence in Macao which began in 1825 and ended when he died there twenty-seven years later.

Memorials of these British residents have survived in Macao, most notably the old East India Company's offices (now a museum) and the tranquil English cemetery which lies below it to the right. Here, against an end wall, is Chinnery's lofty and unfinished tomb. Elsewhere are the graves of such pioneers as Robert Morrison, the clergyman-sinologue who interpreted for the East India Company and translated the Authorized Version of the Bible into Chinese. On the summer's afternoon in which I wandered in this graveyard the heat was intense, and so was the silence. Upon the viridian grass, and along the gravelled paths between the graves, and all over the sarcophagi themselves, the heavy-scented frangipani trees had shed their nubs of pink and white blossom, which you could pick up and sniff at as you walked by. These old English graveyards in the tropics—like, for example, that on Penang Island in Malaya—give you a very sharp and melancholy vision of the hazards to which European lives lay open in the early colonial Empire. The youth, recorded on their tombstones, of many of those buried in such cemeteries seems to emphasize the transient quality of life in a community perpetually threatened by fever and the flux—young husbands, eighteen-year-old brides, and children without number. And yet, in later years, Macao was rated healthier than Hong Kong.

The hydrofoil from Hong Kong took seventy-five minutes to reach Macao. It was one of those strange greenish days which occur in the South China Sea—the islets which we passed were olive-green and the sea like green jade, mottled with dark patches from the reflected clouds. The mouth of the Pearl River and the shallow harbour-water of Macao Bay were, on the other hand, a dull molten-bronze colour, the colour of the river-mud. From the sea, Macao at first appears to consist of a long, low-lying esplanade protected by breakwaters; but once you get into the city you realize that it is built round and upon its seven hills, with very narrow winding streets; a pink stucco Governor's palace; a wealth of baroque churches; shady arcades; gates and overhanging balconies of whorled iron-work; cobblestones; old Portuguese houses; and Chinese shops. On the summit of Penha Hill the Bishop's palace stands in a garden of frangipani and hibiscus and ancient trees that look like green-oaks. From here you can get a bird's-eye, Beatrix Potter view straight down into Communist China. The mouth of the Canton River is flanked by flat, poison-yellow ricefields and the river seems, from here, to be flowing straight out of the distant Chinese mountains. From the same vantage-point you can gaze down on to the tumbled, tiled roofs of Macao city. On the flat rooftops of many of these, long bundles of fireworks were drying, for their manufacture is one of Macao's few export industries. As cheap labour, children are employed in making these fireworks. Later, beneath an archway at the foot of some church steps, we came upon a family group of tiny children, all busily stitching black bugles on to black muslin for mantillas. They seemed as merry as the children of Hong Kong—and probably with as little reason.

While less claustrophobic than Hong Kong Island, the Portuguese Colony of Macao, comprising the city proper, the region between it and the Chinese border, and the two little islands of Colowan and Taipa, is also densely populated. There are almost a quarter of a million Chinese, just over a thousand Portuguese and twenty thousand people of mixed descent, called Macanese. This overwhelming Chinese majority explains the quantity of Buddhist temples, which vie in elaborate grandeur with the rococo churches and convent chapels of the Colony. Two of these are of particular importance, the first being the temple dedicated to A-Ma, the Buddhist goddess of the sea who is worshipped by fishermen and who gave her name to Macao: A-Ma-Kao meaning the Bay of A-Ma. This temple, reputedly of the thirteenth century, looks out over the sea and contains a holy rock on which a fishing junk is carved in bas-relief. The temple courtyard is overshadowed by gnarled trees. Its walls are tiled in green and gold. The second of the great temples is that of the Goddess of Mercy, Kun Yam, and is later in date than the temple of A-Ma. The temple of Kun Yam seems, and perhaps is, the larger of the two. Over its main gateway is a frieze of gods and goddesses. Within the quiet courtyards flowering trees make pools of shade and dappled patterns of sunshine as this comes slanting down. As usual, white and palest pink lotus flowers stand in vases on the main altar in front of the Buddha; in further courts of the temple are other gods and goddesses, twice life-size and ensconced in their own shrines. Shining with scarlet and gold, their faces contorted with snarls of animosity and sheer rage, many of these Macao deities seem even more predatory and alarming than other Chinese gods that I have seen elsewhere. It is no wonder that so much time is spent placating them with offerings and with flowers. Even in the peace of the temple's inner courtyards, and on a day of brilliant sun, they made one wish shiveringly to leave, and to retreat to the winding streets of Portuguese Macao.

The frontier between Macao and China proper is marked by a high, nineteenth-century arched gateway, patrolled on one side by Portuguese sentries, on the farther side by Chinese Communist troops. You reach it down a long straight avenue of banyan trees, and you are not allowed within one hundred yards of the pock-marked, peeling barrier arch. 'The road to China', mournfully remarked the Portuguese girl who was our official guide. On this side of the gate there is, rather symbolically, a coffin-maker's shop. The new coffins (of which a scarcity exists in China) used to be allowed through the gate into Communist territory unopened. Now each has to be opened and inspected by the Communist guards, a duty which, according to Mr Harry Redl, the Canadian photographer of Macao, is regarded as 'both unseemly and unlucky' but which the guards are nevertheless ordered to perform.

The virtual capitulation of Macao to the Communist Chinese in 1967 has meant the swift decline of a city which depended for its main revenues on the tourist trade and on casinos. Few foreigners or Hong Kong Chinese now cross to Macao. To go there that summer was considered daring and almost dangerous. Europeans had been beaten up by Red Guards in the streets, and the British consul made to stand bareheaded in the sun for seven hours. But it seems pointless to travel if you are to be deflected from your goal by considerations of hypothetical risk, and, in fact, on that shimmering day in Macao, nothing remotely disquieting happened at all. The visit also confirmed my own conviction, born many, many years ago amongst the French and British islands of the Caribbean, that a Latin civilization transplants better than an Anglo-Saxon one, though this puzzling fact seems to me almost impossible to explain.

Except for the valleys of the New Territories, there is nothing to vie with the leisurely beauty of Portuguese Macao in the British Crown Colony of Hong Kong.

7

THE STRUGGLE FOR A UNIVERSITY

I

PROTECTED by the bulwark of the New Territories, Hong Kong slid into the new century with colours flying. It was the high noon of Empire, and in the Crown Colony, although Government revenue was insecure, business was thriving. More and more money was being privately made and privately spent, the harbour was fuller of international shipping than ever, construction began on the railway from Kowloon to Canton, and an elaborate road-building programme was devised for the New Territories. The social world now took its tone from Edwardian London and the luxurious standards of entertaining startled visitors as much as the extreme décolletage of the European ladies who, in their enthusiasm for the new fashions, overlooked the effect of the Hong Kong climate on their skin, which one observer described as 'like the skin of an alligator'. Superficially, the world of Hong Kong looked prosperous and smooth: 'the men are all frankly here to make dollars', wrote an Edwardian Governor soon after his arrival, 'and the women to amuse themselves in a reasonable and proper way and both seem to do it with success.'

For the Hong Kong Government, however, there was one problem of increasing seriousness, which was destined to become permanent and to remain insoluble. This was the influx of refugees from China, where in 1911 the Manchu Empire, long disintegrating, finally collapsed, to be succeeded by a disorganized Republic. These refugees naturally demanded housing, food and water, and were devoid of any species of loyalty to the British Colony which was for them merely a convenience and a haven. The population explosion had begun.

All the same, the early twentieth century was marked, for Hong Kong, by a major and long overdue stride forward in education and, in particular, by the laying of the foundation stone, in March 1910, of the University of Hong Kong. This achievement, which was stridently opposed by most of the European business community, was due to the imagination and tenacity of one man—the fourteenth Governor of the Colony, Sir Frederick Lugard, who ruled Hong Kong from 1907 until 1912. 'I am by no means liked here', Lugard once wrote to his wife. 'Even the University scheme which you applaud is unpopular ... never I think in my life have I received such consistently hostile and sneering criticism without even the credit of good intentions.' 'The money-grabbing traders fear that if we educate the Chinaman he may become a serious rival,' Lugard wrote on another occasion. Even the Colonial Office called Lugard's idea for a university for youths from

Anglo-Chinese schools 'Sir Frederick's pet lamb', while the English-language newspapers, as hostile to the Government and as hysterical as ever, attacked the scheme as 'the University fad'. In fact, Hong Kong's debt to Lugard is very considerable. Although a dedicated imperialist, and an admirer and friend of Joseph Chamberlain, he was one of the most open-minded as well as ablest Governors the Crown Colony has yet had.

By the age of forty-nine, when he was appointed to Hong Kong, Lugard had already made his name as a soldier and administrator in Africa, and most recently as High Commissioner for the new Protectorate of Northern Nigeria. He had left Africa, and accepted Hong Kong, chiefly on account of the health of his wife, a distinguished journalist who, before her marriage, had been Colonial Editor of *The Times*. Lugard and his wife had no experience of China or the Chinese, and he had everything to learn about the system of Crown Colony government, which, after the free hand he had had in Nigeria, he found constrictive. Feeling 'horribly circumscribed' he described his role as 'to perpetually functionalize ... to endure fools gladly, to sign my name perpetually and agree to the faultless suggestions of the Honourable the Colonial Secretary.' He disliked the social life of the Colony which, on the other hand, his wife enjoyed. He was a moody and energetic man but, in the words of his biographer, 'like all thoughtful men who have worked on the frontier between West and East, he was forced to recognize the power of the West to destroy the religion and custom of the East without being able to replace them with its own and he saw sheer materialism rushing in to fill the void.' Lugard was against the Christian missionary ideals of education in the East and believed secular morality, if taught properly, to be sufficient. Before he came to Hong Kong he had not, as a matter of fact, thought much about educational theories at all, but he soon found that they interested him 'immensely'. He foresaw a more worthy and ambitious future for Hong Kong than that of being a free port and an international market-place. He wanted it to become 'the Oxford and Cambridge of the Far East'. This was not an ambition with which the foreign business community sympathized.

One of the most remarkable aspects of Frederick Lugard's character was shown in his absolute determination to found the University. Despite the prosperity of the merchants, the Government's revenue was in low water. Moreover, the Chinese population of the Colony had risen by nearly one hundred and fifty thousand in the four years from 1906 to 1910. Two hundred thousand Chinese were crammed into tenements on Hong Kong Island, there were eighty thousand in Kowloon, and a further fifty thousand classified as 'floating'. On the island they were crowded at the rate of a thousand to an acre. The social services were, if anything, more inadequate than ever, for, to get sufficient money for these, trade would have to be heavily taxed, and if this were attempted the traders and their trade would be driven elsewhere. Moreover, the abolition of the opium trade and the closure of the opium dens now ordered by the Liberal Secretary of State for the Colonies, Lord Crewe, involved not only the heavy loss of the revenue from opium but also the payment of compensation to the opium traders. But in spite of these and many other administrative complications, Sir Frederick Lugard stuck to his plans for the Oxford and Cambridge of the East.

In their attitude to the Chinese, of whom, as I have pointed out, they had had no knowledge hitherto, the Lugards were one of the most original couples ever to occupy Government House. Lady Lugard, who, until her health broke down again, overworked herself helping her husband, set aside two hours a day to learn Chinese 'as a relaxation'. They were so impressed by Chinese industry and intelligence that they even began to consider whether the yellow races might not in fact be superior to the white races. Lady Lugard thought that they were superior; her husband agreed that the worst Europeans were far below the worst orientals, but maintained that the best Europeans were better than the best of the yellow races. They admired the Tung Wah Hospital, which Lady Lugard called extremely dainty and elegant'. The Governor did his best to make contact with the committee of the hospital and with the other committees formed by local Chinese merchants for charitable and social work. He found, as other Governors had found before him, that Government House tended to be insulated from the Chinese: 'I am not sufficiently in touch—personal touch—with them,' he complained. He even thought that the future of the world might one day depend upon the Chinese: 'Truly', he wrote, 'I often wonder whether the dream of the Yellow Peril is not likely to come true some day, and the Chinaman by sheer ability and industry will dominate the commerce of the world.' He paid a state visit to the Viceroy at Canton and received him in return at Government House. It was this intelligent interest in everything Chinese which inspired Lugard's conception of a university which should offer a first-class scientific Western education to Chinese students.

II

To get the University project going proved, as might be expected, a highly uphill task. An aged Parsee named Hormusjee Mody came forward with an offer of slightly less than £18,000 to inaugurate a fund to build the University. This seemed a good start, but disappointment followed. The British merchant community remained tepid about the scheme, when they were not definitely hostile to it, and at first would contribute no money to the fund. It was not till Lady Lugard, back in London, canvassed the offices of the big Hong Kong firms that Butterfield and Swire, and the China Association, gave £40,000 each and other contributions began to seep slowly in. Nor was opposition merely local; in 1909 the United Universities Scheme had been launched in Great Britain to establish a university at Hankow, with the aid of British universities and religious bodies. This scheme, especially in its emphasis on Christian teaching and the humanities, would have rendered Lugard's own project abortive. The leader of the movement, Lord William Cecil, regarded Lugard's ideas as irreligious and full of danger: 'Young men, yellow or white,' he wrote, 'are enthusiastic and must have great causes put before them; we Christians put before them the higher moral tone of the individual. A merely Utilitarian University leaves to a great extent the enthusiasm of youth unoccupied and therefore it becomes a hotbed of revolutionary intrigue.' As much as any retrograde British merchant in Hong Kong, Lord William was alarmed by the project: ' ... two ideas will probably fill your University' he wrote in another letter. 'Number one, China for the Chinese and death to the foreigners; number two, the equality of man and its two developments, socialism and anarchism ... to foster a crowd of bomb-throwing patriots in your midst will be extremely unpleasant.'

An important part of Lugard's scheme was to ask the Peking Government for some financial support. He approached them through the British ambassador at Peking. They agreed, but on condition that they could send an Inspector of Schools to Hong Kong. Here Lugard offended not only the Colonial Office but the Foreign Office too. The latter declared that a Governor of Hong Kong had no right to make a direct approach to the Chinese Government through the British ambassador; he should have first asked the Colonial Office, who would then have asked the Foreign Office who might then have sent instructions to the ambassador. The Colonial Office, in any case, were against Chinese participation, because it went counter to their traditional policy of keeping Chinese influence out of Hong Kong. Categorizing Lugard's request to the British ambassador as 'an extraordinarily ill-judged proceeding', the Colonial Office ordered him to get the British ambassador in Peking to cancel the negotiations, and to refuse the money which the Chinese had already promised to give. This action humiliated Lugard, offended the Chinese, and embarrassed the ambassador. 'This is the way', commented Lugard, 'our C.O. helps the man on the spot.' In the end the Chinese Government were allowed to contribute the modest sum of £25,000 with no conditions attached. Great Britain's contribution to the founding of Hong Kong University was a derisory grant of £300 a year, to be called King Edward VII Scholarships, a bursary which is said to have made Sir Frederick Lugard blush.

III

After Lugard had left Hong Kong, his University struggled on. Money was short and so was staff; the indifference of the British business community continued, but successive Governors managed to make the University small grants. During the Japanese invasion of 1941 the University buildings were virtually destroyed. Hong Kong University has not yet fulfilled Lugard's conception of an Oxford and Cambridge of the East and, indeed, even as recently as 1957 there were less than one thousand students. Two years ago the number had risen to more than two thousand, and it is hoped that by 1970 there will be two thousand seven hundred and fifty. The University continues to cater mostly for pupils from Anglo-Chinese schools and the teaching is in English. In 1963 another university was inaugurated—the federal-type Chinese University of Hong Kong with Chinese as the principal language. This University has an undergraduate enrolment of almost two thousand, and is to be beautifully sited at Sha Tin in the New Territories.

The story of Lugard's University emphasizes, if that were needed, the extreme difficulty of getting a purely commercial society interested in cultural and intellectual values and, indeed, in any activity which is not visibly and immediately a source of financial gain. There have been no

Medici or Fuggers in the history of British Hong Kong. But Lugard's aim of teaching young Chinese how British ideas and inventions worked from the inside has clearly been successful. In an often-quoted address given by Dr Sun Yat-sen to Hong Kong University in 1923, the great revolutionary leader paid tribute to what he had learned there: 'That is the answer to the question "Where did I get my revolutionary ideas from?" It was entirely from Hong Kong.' When he had left Hong Kong after taking a degree at the Medical College there he 'began to wonder how it was that foreigners, that Englishmen, could do such things as they have done, for example, with the barren rock of Hong Kong within seventy or eighty years, while in four thousand years China had no place like Hong Kong.' He urged the students he was addressing to learn by English examples, and to spread their experience and knowledge to every part of China. In a strange manner these sentiments of Sun Yat-sen seem to justify both Sir Frederick Lugard and his opponents at the same time.

EPILOGUE

I

FOR Hong Kong, the most noticeable effect of those revolutionary ideas which Sun Yat-sen had imbibed at its new University was an ever-increasing flow of refugees into the Colony, reaching tidal-wave proportions after the outbreak of the Sino-Japanese War in 1937. These refugees, whose chief contribution to Hong Kong was epidemics of smallpox and cholera, formed the main problem with which the Government had to cope during the Colony's somewhat uneventful history in the 'twenties and 'thirties of this century.

That most gratuitous of all international holocausts, the First World War, had made no immediately visible impact upon the Colony. Rich people subscribed to war charities. A large sum of money was raised and dutifully given to the British Government. Immediately after the war, however, Hong Kong life was disrupted by strikes, culminating in the seamen's strike of 1922 which put the harbour temporarily out of action and ended by infecting all Chinese workers, including those in private or domestic service. In the same year the shape of things to come was foreshadowed by a clause in the Washington Treaties between Great Britain, the United States and Japan which limited by ratio the size of the fleets of these three nations, but even so left Japan the most powerful naval force in the Pacific. By another clause of the treaties it was agreed that no more fortifications should be built in British, American or Japanese possessions east of the 110th meridian which runs through Java, Borneo and Hainan. Hong Kong, already fairly indefensible, was thus left virtually defenceless.

Meanwhile, in Great Britain, the rise of the Labour Party, and the general post-war disenchantment, began to make the very notion of a Colonial Empire lose its sheen. Already, in its Benthamite conception, out of date, the Crown Colony of Hong Kong became increasingly a complete anachronism. The new British emphasis on welfare and social services was not reflected in the Colony, although an ordinance was at least passed in 1923 to try to protect Chinese children employed in factories, and, as late as 1938, a Labour Officer was finally appointed to deal with labour disputes. When, in 1931, Great Britain went off the gold standard, abandoning free trade for imperial preference, Hong Kong remained a free port in an Empire now dedicated to protection. The Colony's reaction to this confusing and anomalous position was a new emphasis on home industries as against entrepôt trade. To shipbuilding, always Hong Kong's leading industry, was now added the manufacture of textiles, and of articles as diverse as rattan furniture and flashlight batteries, rubber shoes and firecrackers and scent. With the construction of the airfield at Kai Tak, Hong Kong quickly became the most important air terminal in the West Pacific; and you could now, if you so wished, travel all the way to Europe from Kowloon by train.

EPILOGUE

In 1938 the Japanese seizure of Canton during the opening months of their war with China brought Japanese Imperial troops right up to the borders of the New Territories, causing the refugee problem to take on sinister proportions for Hong Kong. All the same, whilst the presence of a Japanese army on the very frontier inspired some Hong Kong residents with a sense of doom not unlike that to be found in the sagas of Tolkien, life in the Colony remained normal and business throbbed away as usual. So far Hong Kong, for all its contentious social history, had led a charmed life. Nothing worse than occasional, but devastating, typhoons or an epidemic of plague had ever really struck the Colony. And then, on the morning of December 8th, 1941, the people of Hong Kong Island were disturbed at breakfast-time by the echoes of thunderous explosions from Kowloon-side, across the harbour. Although some of them had just heard on their radios the news of the Japanese victory at Pearl Harbour, they did not at first connect these unusual reverberations with the outbreak of a war. It was not until ominous plumes of blackish smoke were seen rising from the airport at Kai Tak that they realized that, for the first time in its history, Hong Kong was under attack. Simultaneously two Japanese divisions crossed the border into the New Territories and swept down on Kowloon, which was captured six days later. The massive shelling of the city of Victoria, backed up by aerial and naval bombardment, began. Seventeen days later, on a Christmas Day just one century after the foundation of the Crown Colony, Hong Kong's twenty-first Governor, Sir Mark Young, was compelled to surrender it to Lieutenant-General Sakai, the commander of the

Japanese invading force. Sir Mark Young was imprisoned in the Peninsula Hotel at Kowloon, while all other foreigners, civilian and military alike, were herded into a concentration camp at Stanley, high up above the shining blue waters of Tai Tam Bay. For three days and nights the city of Victoria was brutally put to the sack. It is estimated that more than ten thousand Chinese and Eurasian women of all ages were subjected during this period to multiple rape, and those hospitals still functioning treated them not only for the effects of this, but for broken noses, smashed teeth, and bayonet wounds. Such was Hong Kong's introduction to rule by fellow-Asiatics.

II

The official explanation of the series of lightning victories won by Japan in the Far East during 1941 and 1942 is that they held the initiative; and this is, in itself, true. Air Chief Marshal Sir Robert Brooke-Popham, the unfortunate British Commander-in-Chief in the Far East, was instructed from London by telegram: 'Avoidance of war with Japan is basis of Far East policy and provocation must be rigidly avoided.' A Chiefs-of-Staff directive of August 1940 reminded him that 'our policy in the Far East is still to avoid war with Japan'. But it would seem legitimate to suggest that there was another reason—that consistent contempt for Asiatic races which made the British, like the Dutch and the Americans, grossly underestimate the power, the strategy and the tactics of the Japanese. Brooke-Popham, for instance, was advised that the Japanese could not attack several places at once—that they might attack Hong Kong, or Malaya, or the Philippines, but never, as in fact happened, all three areas simultaneously. It was also assumed that the Japanese army could not land on beaches in bad weather and that their fighter aircraft were, by European standards, inferior. The long range, speed, and manoeuvrability of the Zero fighters therefore came as a nasty shock. So did the mobility of the Japanese army, which depended less on mechanization than did the British, could live off the country, required only simple food, in its Spartan way needed no comforts and operated with total flexibility. What Brooke-Popham later described as 'the individual initiative of the Japanese soldier' was another source of amazement of British officers.

What was believed by the Commander-in-Chief at his headquarters in Singapore was naturally accepted by those under his command. Thus Major-General Maltby, who organized the dismayingly brief and unsuccessful defence of Hong Kong, was convinced, up to the moment when Japanese troops flowed into the New Territories and Kai Tak airport was bombed, that the Japanese were bluffing and would never declare war upon the Allied powers. General Maltby had also been informed that Japanese night-work was poor, that the Japanese 'preferred stereotyped methods and fixed plans', that Japanese automatics were not as 'numerous as ours nor so up to date', that the Japanese air force was not up to first-class European standards, that their bombing was poor and that they could never indulge in night bombing. He was likewise led to believe that although their combined operations might be thorough, the spectacular Japanese successes against the Chinese army 'were flattering as there had never been real opposition.' In fact, the Japanese troops who attacked Hong

Kong and who had undergone a month's intensive training in fighting by night in order to invade the New Territories, proved full of surprises. They often wore quilted material with cross-stitching into which twigs and grass could be inserted for camouflage, or carried camouflage nets on their backs. Their boots had rubber soles, they could swim fully armed at night, their snipers and scouts were highly trained and almost impossible to detect. Their light mortars were perilously effective and exact in aim, and the Japanese aerial bombing was devastating and precise. Both in Hong Kong and in Malaya Japanese troops were guided by fifth columnists, and were in any case equipped with the best and most detailed British maps of the territories. In Malaya they also showed an ability 'to cross natural obstacles, i.e. rivers, swamps, thick jungle etc., much more rapidly than had been thought possible'. It was all rated rather horrible—and not in the least what British officers had been led to expect from little yellow people who still believed in the tea ceremony and had a contemptible passion for chrysanthemums and azaleas.

The apathy or, worse still, the disloyalty of subject races, who were not, in Hong Kong, especially interested in protecting European wealth, or, in Malaya, in saving rubber plantations and tin mines to help the British war effort, was especially disappointing to their defenders. The Chinese and Malays proved unexpectedly brave under fire, but drivers would disappear, dock workers slip away without any warning whatever. In Malaya, as in Hong Kong, the preferential treatment given to British women and children in war-time did not inspire orientals with respect. In Hong Kong almost all British women and children had been skilfully evacuated during the summer of 1941; the same happened on Penang Island in Malaya, where even the wives of the Sikh police were left behind. Many Eurasian and Chinese ladies had worked side by side with European women in essential defence services, and the former could see no reason why they themselves could not be evacuated too. Lieutenant-General Perceval, who presided over the military collapse of Malaya, was well aware of this and took the view that racial preference in evacuation plans would 'clearly be little short of disastrous' and 'a severe blow to British prestige'.

> Although Japan's policy was to try to rally all Asiatics to her flag with the cry of 'Asia for the Asiatics' [he wrote] our political object was clearly to hold Malaya for the British Empire ... If, therefore, we evacuated immediately all European women, leaving Eurasian and Asiatic women to do their work, we should, it seemed, be playing into the hands of the Japanese and provide fertile ground for the seeds of their propaganda.

In the end, in Singapore, it was decided to give all nationalities wishing to leave impartial treatment. But then arose the thorny question of where evacuated Asiatics were to go? Finally Australia, which had welcomed British women and children with cups of tea and open arms, reluctantly agreed to accept fifteen hundred female Chinese.

III

We have seen that, owing to a clause in the Washington Treaties of 1922, Hong Kong could have no modern defences. Why, then, was it defended at all? In his retrospective dispatch on the loss of Malaya, Sir Robert Brooke-Popham explained that 'Hong Kong was regarded officially as an undesirable military commitment, or else as an outpost to be held as long as possible.' The two reasons which, he asserted, had influenced the decision not to demilitarize Hong Kong were, firstly, its possible effect on the morale and war effort of the Chinese administration of Chiang Kai-shek and, secondly, because of what the United States might or might not think or do. Up till the middle of 1941 the British did not know whether the Americans would or would not defend the Philippines were they attacked. It was argued that if we, so to say, abandoned Hong Kong, the Americans might be influenced to withdraw from the Philippines, cease to take any direct interest in the Far East 'and confine themselves to the eastern half of the Pacific.' And so Hong Kong, with an inadequate garrison, and provisioned both in military stores and food reserves for one hundred and thirty days, became a hostage to fortune. The garrison at the outbreak of war consisted of one battalion of the Middlesex Regiment, one battalion of the Royal Scots, two newly arrived and rawly trained battalions of Canadian troops, and two Indian battalions. The total strength of all personnel on December 8th, 1941, was just over fourteen and a half thousand. No air forces had been allotted to the defence of the Colony, the naval units were weak, the anti-aircraft guns few, and there was no radar equipment. To economize on manpower the defending forces were diluted 'by Chinese personnel of unknown reliability in war-time' and there was no regular transport driven by disciplined drivers. The vast Chinese civilian population formed an unknown quantity at the outbreak of war and considerably impeded operations once the invasion had got under way. True to their traditions, armed gangs of robbers now invaded the air-raid shelters and tunnels, in defiance of all police efforts to combat them. Rice distribution proved more and more difficult. Water, naturally, began to run out when the Japanese either bombed or captured reservoirs. Major-General Maltby had, in fact, an impossible task, and so indeed did the Governor, Sir Mark Young, who, on December 21st, received a stirring signal from Winston Churchill: 'Resist to the end'.

The defence of Hong Kong had been planned with a view to holding out on the mainland as long as possible, and then deftly withdrawing to the island. With the purpose of delaying the enemy in the New Territories a series of defensive positions had been prepared and were known as the Gin Drinkers' Line. This was, in theory, a strong line of defence and a great deal of work had been done on it, but it would have needed two or more divisions to hold it. It extended along a front of ten and a half miles, but had little depth and contained two dangerous passes. The Japanese, who invaded the Colony with two complete divisions and a third one held in reserve, turned this line in the first twenty-four hours, and swept down on Kowloon, from which the British, Canadian and Indian troops were being evacuated. There was hand-to-hand fighting on the quayside as the loaded ferries left with the last troops for Hong Kong Island.

On the morning of December 13th, a launch bearing a flag of truce was seen putting off from Kowloon. A Japanese staff officer stepped ashore at Victoria Pier bringing a letter to the Governor from Lieutenant-General Sakai. This demanded the surrender of the Colony, 'and threatened severe artillery fire and aerial bombardment in the event of refusal.' With one of those Churchillian gestures which usually cost thousands of lives, Sir Mark Young rejected this demand, and a similar request some days later. On December 16th 'a prominent Chinese merchant' was arrested for defeatist talk. This was considered to have had 'a salutary effect'. During the night of December 18th – 19th the first Japanese landings were made on Hong Kong Island. To raise morale a communiqué was issued by the Government that Chiang Kai-shek was sending troops for the relief of the Colony. By this time Victoria was subjected to heavy bombing and to shelling described as as bad as anything on the Western Front in the 1914–18 war. The island's defences had also been shelled, fifth columnists guided the enemy along remote tracks on the mountain-sides, whilst others signalled across the harbour at night with mirrors and primitive lamps. Any of these who were caught were summarily shot.

Once fighting had begun on the island itself, a Japanese victory was inevitable. The defending troops fought on with a hopeless courage, suffering from exhaustion, the wet and cold at night, absence of hot food and absence of ammunition. The gardens of fine villas were soon littered with putrefying military corpses, and in the Repulse Bay Hotel the remaining European women and children crouched on the floor of the main saloon as the Japanese attacked. On Christmas Day, as we have seen, Hong Kong surrendered.

IV

The four-year occupation of Hong Kong by the Japanese settled down into an orderly reign of terror, with brothel areas for the troops cordoned off in Victoria. It is strange that the Japanese, at home so considerate and civilized a race, should, as conquerors, have proved both bestial and stupid. In the case of Hong Kong, in particular, with its huge Chinese population whose loyalty to the British was never whole-hearted, it seems equally odd that the conquerors should not have tried to woo rather than to alienate and terrorize the Chinese inhabitants. Under their rule the population of Hong Kong dwindled, but amongst the Chinese and Eurasians who remained were many who showed extraordinary examples of courage under torture and the threat of death. In August 1945 the British once again took the Crown Colony and rehabilitation swiftly and efficiently began.

Looking at Hong Kong today, it is as hard to believe in the atrocities of the Japanese as it is to accept the fact that this teeming metropolitan island was, not so very long ago, a bleak and barren rock. British historians of this Crown Colony never tire of reminding us that it is a uniquely British achievement. It seems to me, on the other hand, to be just as much the achievement of that astounding, intelligent and persevering race which generations of British colonists have treated with a smug tolerance: the ordinary Hong Kong Chinese.

What is it, I have often wondered while writing this book, that fundamentally affronts me about this Crown Colony, so oddly reputed sensual and exotic, in actual fact so harsh and so banal? It is not only the historical, arrogant attitude of the British—for, as it happened, the attitude of the Imperial Chinese to all other races was, if possible, even more disdainful. Is it that, like Lady Lugard, I suspect the orientals of being superior to the people of the West? Is it a natural distaste for the pursuit of money as an end in itself? I think, rather, that it is that Hong Kong, like many of its own products, is a commercial artifact, and bears the indelible and vulgar hallmark imposed on the East by the West. I do not pretend to have an understanding of the Chinese character, but what I believe I do possess is an admiration for its humanity and its traditional values. That great, and now well-nigh forgotten, interpreter of the West to the East, Lafcadio Hearn, once wrote, in a letter of 1893, that he feared that the Japanese of the next generation 'will not be kind and open-hearted and unselfish ... they will become hard of character like the Western people—more intellectual and less moral. For old Japan, in character, was as far in advance of the West as she was materially behind it.' He was writing of Japan, but his words might apply to any Eastern community which has been subjected to the perverting interests and obsessions of Western commerce. It is my view that it could be applied to the atmosphere and ethos of Hong Kong, a place where Chinese good nature is exploited daily.

The chronic water-shortage on Hong Kong Island has made the state of the reservoirs ever a dominant conversational theme. The reservoir which is not mentioned is that into which generations of Hong Kong Europeans have happily and profitably dipped their scoops—the reservoir of the underhoused, the impoverished and the unemployed.

A SELECT BIBLIOGRAPHY OF PUBLISHED SOURCES

E. J. Eitel, *Europe in China. The history of Hong Kong from the beginning to the year 1882* (Hong Kong, 1895).
G. B. Endacott, *A History of Hong Kong* (Oxford University Press, 1958).
Mrs Thomas Brassey, *A Voyage in the 'Sunbeam'* (Longmans, Green & Co., 1878).
Maurice Collis, *Foreign Mud: Being an Account of the Opium Imbroglio at Canton in the 1830's* (Faber & Faber, 1946).
Austin Coates, *Prelude to Hong Kong* (Routledge & Kegan Paul, 1966).
G. R. Sayer, *Hong Kong, Birth, Adolescence and Coming of Age* (Oxford University Press, 1937).
H. Ingrams, *Hong Kong* (H.M.S.O., London, 1952).
T. F. Ryan, S. J., *The Story of a Hundred Years: The Pontifical Institute of Foreign Missions in Hong Kong, 1858–1958* (Hong Kong, 1959).
Sir Charles Jeffries, *The Colonial Office* (Allen & Unwin, 1956).
F. D. Ommanney, *Fragrant Harbour: A Private View of Hong Kong* (Hutchinson, 1962).

Li Shu-Fan, *Hong Kong Surgeon* (Victor Gollancz, 1964).

Hong Kong Report for the Year 1966 (Hong Kong Government Press, 1967).

The Hong Kong General Chamber of Commerce, 1966: Annual Report (Hong Kong, 1967).

H. Smith, *John Stuart Mill's Other Island: A Study of the economic development of Hong Kong* (Institute of Economic Affairs Research Monographs no. 6: I.E.A., London, 1966).

M. G. Whissen, *Under the Rug: the Drug Problem in Hong Kong* (Printed for the Hong Kong Council of Social Services, 1965).

Use has also been made of the memoirs of Sir John Bowring, Sir William des Voeux, Lord Ronald Gower and Miss Isabella Bird, as well as of the private papers of Sir John Pope Hennessy.